A COUNTR. . .

RHYMES

and

VERSES

from an

EAST ANGLIAN COUNTRY POET

DICK GIBSON

A COUNTRY POET

First published in 2018 by

THE ERSKINE PRESS, THE WHITE HOUSE, ECCLES, NORWICH NR16 2PB

WWW.ERSKINE-PRESS.COM

ISBN 978 1 85297 123 6

Typeset by Esme Power

Printed and bound in Great Britain by 4edge Ltd, Hockley

Aiding East Anglian Childrens Hospice

Dick Gibson

Born in 1937 of Scots parentage spent the first third of his life at Frowick Hall St Osyth in North East Essex on the family dairy farm, moving to Frenze near Diss in 1973, an Essex man in Norfolk for many years, now a Norfolk man from Essex, a cattle enthusiast all his life but especially dairy cattle stopped active management of cows in 1988 to become involved in advising and selling dairy cattle genetics across the Southern and Eastern Counties of England, and retains an active involvement in the local dairy cattle breeding clubs in E Anglia to this day.

Likes a bit of scribbling and hopes he can give you a smile or even a thought.

The EAST ANGLIAN CHILDRENS HOSPICE

Like most folks there are many charities that touch my heart with many people suffering, but none more so than EACH, as one who has been fortunate to go through life without any illnesses my heart truly goes out to those young children who are suffering with debilitating and life threatening illnesses at such an early age and are denied the opportunities the majority of us take as our right. It is also fair to remember that their parents are in the early stages of their own lives and have not had the opportunities to build up the financial reserves needed to survive in the way those taken ill in their retirement have had. If my effort's with this book aids EACH which is part of our local community with their funds my scribbling will not be in vain.

EACH

EACH cares for children and young people with life threatening conditions across Cambridgeshire, Essex, Norfolk and Suffolk, EACH hospice's are places where families feel safe, at home and they can spend quality time together; enabling parents to be parents and not care givers.

EACH is reliant on donations for the majority of their income.

With many thanks to Lucinda Morgan, a leading pedigree livestock photographer, for permission to use the cover photograph. (info@lucindamorgan.co.uk), and thanks to The Erskine Press for their help and assistance in the preparation and production of this book.

COUNTRY KIDDIE

Born and bred a country kiddie
No doubt from day one that's what I would be
Never would I grasp the eloquence of suburban charm
Always favouring the rural influence of a farm
Should anyone question the validity of my rural roots
Take a downward glance at the mud on my boots
A youthful existence in fields
and by hedgerows all day long
Dominated by sounds of animals, tractors and birdsong
Right enough I went to school and did my learning
But cows, pigs, sheep and crops that was my yearning
Yes a born and bred countryman through and through
I have had other interests but that is all I really knew
Just like the other's I set aside time for leisure
Hunting, shooting and fishing amongst those giving pleasure
Satisfaction gained from working with pigs, sheep or a cow
With few scenes equalling that of seagulls following the plough
The barn owl, the hawk hovering or a heron in flight
What value can you put on such a country sight
Hearing a woodpecker pecking at a tree is a welcome sound
Or seeing it on a lawn foraging for ants or insects on the ground
Moles to voles and other creatures living in holes even bumble bees
No need to mention birds nesting and squirrels running up trees
An everyday observer of seasons and nature at its core
Relating and appreciating so much of country folklore
A country kiddie that's all I ever wanted to be
But now a country oldie with a countryside memory.

TITCHMARSH DISEASE

Oh! The multitude of folks in the land with Titchmarsh disease
To be seen in gardens pulling weeds on their hands and knees
Some retired thinking life should be as if to the manor born
Instead of forever hoeing or mowing the lawn
Ensuring that hanging baskets are fertilised and well fed
Never mentioning watering when they are above the head
Sufferers seen at garden centres regardless of the cost
Loading up their cars with bags and bags of compost
The vegetable garden continually being dug and manured
Coming second to that roadside hedge meticulously manicured
The green house with seeds planted and sprouted sitting in trays
Just waiting for spring and some frost free days
Younger folk landscaping gardens with patios, shrubs and trees
Signalling the early onset of Titchmarsh disease
Vegetables neatly planted and spaced in regulated rows
Peas, beans, carrots, cabbages, potatoes, cucumbers and marrows
Scents and perfumes that stimulate and tantalise noses
Sprays for green fly and black fly that may attack roses
Secure in the knowledge that everything will be alright in June
Having long since checked the optimum time to prune
Shrubs and borders laid out with a colourful view
From spring to summer and autumn right the way through
From first thing in the morning after getting out of bed
Backwards and forward from garden to greenhouse and potting shed
In some of the worst case scenarios of Titchmarsh disease
People have bought chainsaws to lop branches off trees.

STAG OAK

If only that stag oak on the horizon could tell its story
Now aged over hundreds of years it stands with regal glory
There it stands on the skyline majestic and serene
Part of my never ending Norfolk country scene
One can only guess which century would have seen its birth
Some may make calculations based on its substantial girth
Likely to have been there before Lord Raleigh laid down his cloak
Always a heart-warming sight to see such a wonderful oak
Through the many hot summers and winters it has known
One can wonder and ask how many tons of acorns it has grown
What number of birds have chosen it as a place to nest
The multitude of new born chicks it has blessed
Over centuries to man and beast it has given aid
With shelter from storms and in hot sun, some shade
A sentinel in the sky, its uppermost branches continually bare
Although lower branches fully leaved, plenty of life still there
Oh! If it could only relate the changes it has seen
As it looks to houses standing, where once fields were green
If asked would it prefer the tranquillity of yesterday
Rather than the fear of someone wanting to build a motorway
Congratulations to the conservationists who fight with their might
To preserve that stag oak, a beautiful and serene sight.

RUSTIC RONNIE

Rustic Ronnie in and out between showers
Tending to his vegetables and flowers
Vegetables planted with military precision standing in rows
Flowers planted more imaginatively ensuring colour flows
The striped lawn meticulously cut and edged
The hedge spikey unable to cut it till birds have fledged
Always taking pride never regarding it as a toil
Digging and fertilizing keen to improve the garden soil
Never bothered by computers or a mobile phone
It was the garden or allotment that set the tone
Sometimes some sea angling for a bit of sport
His wife encouraged to cook whatever he caught
Beating on nearby estates during the shooting season
Company of others and being close to nature the reason
Having always regarded shooting as good fun
Others judging him as a pretty fair shot with a gun
Always in his element and never far away
If anywhere near there was a vintage ploughing match day
Without his own tractor and plough unable to compete
Pleasure gained from fellow countrymen he would meet
A complete intolerance of any garden pests and weeds
Every step taken to ensure maximum progress for his seeds
Always competitive ready and willing to have a go
Planting dates judged as best for the local horticultural show
Always prudent ensuring nothing was ever lost
Moved plants into the greenhouse ahead of the first frost
Only once was Ronnie known to look forlorn
When a mole had the audacity to come up on his lawn.

HOITY TOITY

Oh! What changed that comely wench
I once sat beside on a park bench
Full of humour who would play with any kiddie
Now a humourless self-centred old biddy
She may tell you the good she and her family do
But not one question does she ask about you
Showing no interest in what may be your story
Preoccupied by her own status and glory
Content that she is one of those few
For whom only the better things will do
Everything designed for those she wishes to impress
Whether it be house, garden, shoes or dress
Carefully choosing those she wants to greet
Ensuring associations are with those considered elite
Accustomed to the trappings of upper class life
Having had the good fortune of a wealthier life
Superiority dominating her mind and thought
Created in part by success in those fields of sport
Taking care to not be judged with local allsorts
Having only indulged in the upper class sports
Be advised not to question an opinion she has expressed
She knows it is not only right, but the best
Oh! How those delusions of grandeur exude
What changed that comely lass, into a prude?
Now no resemblance to the comely wench
I once sat beside on a park bench.

Written after meeting an early girlfriend unseen for over fifty years.

THE GARDEN

Oh! Why did I make that declaration of intent
That above all others my garden would be resplendent
A rake a watering can a garden hose
All necessary equipment for vegetables in regimental rows
Hours spent with careful determination on, propagation
And await a multitude of plants in proliferation
Soil lavished with compost and manure
My plants will be better than those in the glossy brochure
Every year new plants and shrubs to buy
With fancy colours to please the eye.
Deterrents for lily beetle, green and black fly
Amongst a host of other things I have to buy
Rose bushes and shrubs that I carefully prune
To ensure that I have a worthy spectacle in June
Sadly the frost got the grapes growing on the vine
"Best buy them!" Compressed into a bottle of "Wine".
Oh! Why don`t, I just lie in bed?
Because there are lawns to mow and flowers to dead head
How much simpler life would be
If I just sat watching racing, antiques and other twaddle on TV
Dandy lions, thistles, nettles and brambles growing unrestricted
If I decided to be no longer garden addicted
To hang with you rabbits and moles
Just carry on digging your miserable holes
Oh! How much simpler life will be
Half a day with a chain saw and a strimmer, that's Me.

WOMEN

Why do women think it is not their duty to mow the lawn
Yet always aspire to see it striped and closely shorn
Preferring to vacuum and keep the house clean
Taking care not to let her man near the washing machine
All garden and power tools get a man`s complete reliance
Yet displays distrust if a man operates a domestic appliance
Even though a plumbing or electrical repair
Is best left to a husband, neighbour or a son and heir
Drilling a hole in the wall to fix a screw
That is another job women are unwilling to do.
Women hang curtains but men put up the poles
Women buy flowers and garden plants and men dig the holes
Inside the house furniture and fashion the woman`s choice
Much as a man may express his opinion, he has no voice
Yes the woman`s prerogative to choose the decor
But a man gets to do the messy parts of the chore
House or garden women select pastel shades that tone and blend
Men totally oblivious for fear of the money they will spend
She relies on men to open and shut doors and change the clocks
But woe betide him if he goes near her needlework box.
It is the woman`s choice that plans the family diet
Whether fancied or not he is unwise not to try it
A women will cook sumptuous desserts that are sublime
A man depended on to provide a complimentary wine
For women shopping, a challenge even if nothing is bought
Reckoned better than a Saturday afternoon watching sport
A woman`s car quiet comfortable and clean
A man`s choice either a functional or more prestigious machine
Claims diamonds and jewellery are rewards for loyalty and trust
To men, honest recognition of inconsiderate selfishness and lust.

THE RIVER WAVENEY

An artery running out from East Anglia`s heart
For many miles keeping Norfolk and Suffolk apart
Rising in Redgrave Fen, that is it`s source
Beginning as a stream, but soon gaining force
On a sometimes torturous fifty mile route to the sea
Mills for both corn and cloth, now consigned to history.
Flowing freely unhindered on its own accord
Past Diss joined by the Frenze on its way to Billingford
Then the Dove before Syleham, Brockdish and Needham
To Weybread past the Pits to Munnings birthplace, Mendham
Through places of infinite beauty and idyllic charm
Some secluded, only indicated as a name to a farm.
Forever gaining strength as it makes its way
Through Wortwell , Homersfield and Earsham to Bungay
Regardless of however much rain
The river meadows are the Waveney`s flood plain
Twists and turns at Ditchingham onto the old mill at Ellingham
Which I believe eclipses the one better hidden at Needham
Through the wide expanse of river meadows to Geldeston
With its pub, and on towards Beccles the river flows incessantly on.
With every turn, new vistas unfold
Scenes of tranquil beauty many as yet untold
The river only navigable as far as Geldeston lock
Beccles the gateway to the Broads where tourists flock
Now greater expanses of water more open planned
As it embraces the leisure spirit of Broadland.
Holiday makers unhurried with time to spare
Some with motor cruisers hired up on the Yare
The river forever getting wider and deeper
As it passes the moorings at Burgh St Peter

Past Somerleyton`s swing bridge and on up to St Olaves
Where the railway runs alongside passengers give waves
Across Fritton marshes continuing on the journey
To Breydon Water joining the Yare, before the sea.

ORGANIC ?

It might be a thought, if you think it through
With water from the well, and still an outside loo
They spread it onto the garden to make vegetables grow
Now chemically in supermarkets at a few pence a throw
In years gone by it was that outside loo
Not chemicals, and how those veggies grew
Oh! Was it the digging in of that human waste
That provided them with that country fresh taste
That human mixture of pee and poo
Unbelievable what in a garden that could do
With only human, horse or farmyard manure to fertilize
Ensuring that vegetables grew quickly to the right size
No matter what.   Carrots, onions and cabbages too
Everything benefitted with soil enriched with residue
Soil that was prepared and cultivated without panic
For vegetables now commanding a premium as organic
There is no doubt, that which was known as the privy
Was the one in the garden providing the biggest divi.

PAUL KNIGHTS

Never one to be checked or kept in hand
That was Paul Knights from Kessingland
Where ever you have met him, give him his due
He was a Suffolk born character through and through
Abrasive, cheeky and tough, as hard as a rock
Befitting descendents from fishing and life boatman stock
Not for him a future based on the sea and sand
Wishing to make his living from animals and the land
Two years national service with ambitions fraught
Yet lifelong friendships made with boxing his sport.
Now determined to become a master of the soil
Enlisting a wife, Kathleen to help him in his toil
Settling down with no inclination to rove
Working for some time with Robbie at South Cove
Until the opportunity arose to chance his own arm
Moving to Stow Bedon and taking on Church Farm
Intensive with cows and pigs for a farm its size
Pigs good enough to win the Smithfield Fat-stock prize
Now with a young family and their future to secure
Canada away from nuclear fear and great cows was the lure.
With livestock machinery and furniture all dispersed
To Fergus Ontario for a life completely un-rehearsed
Yet one animal remaining to bring eternal fame
Kessingland Ella won the Royal and everybody knew the name
Adjusting to Canadian ways and farming practices was the thing
Socially,   Sarah, Alice and Toby soon getting into the swing
The Toronto Winter Fair and visitors from England
Fostering those deep rooted memories of Kessingland
A man of diverse thoughts, knowing how to work his ticket
He welcomed the chance to be bag carrier for Claude Picket.
Oh! How he relished visiting his homeland shores

Lucky to have Kathleen and the girls to do the chores
If frequent visits to England were to be his quest
Time to put his skills at cattle marketing to the test
British breeders hungry for the best Holsteins to be found
He an enthusiastic Englishman was there on the ground
With the eyes and ears to meet their need
Whether it was show cows or deep pedigreed
Cattle bought and sold meeting every desire
Until his quarantine barn was mysteriously burnt by fire.
With forces at work beyond his control
Time for new challenges in a different role
Embarking on a new career determined by fate
A business consultant with Alice in real estate
Time erasing English mud from his boots
With five grandchildren establishing Canadian roots
Retired and living in a street with an Irish flavour
But still with thoughts of East Anglia to savour
One wonders who dealt such an interesting hand
To Paul Knights a Suffolk boy from Kessingland.

TAIL-END CHARLIE

Long gone the days of energy forever more
With challenges of work and emotion at the fore
Gone the day`s when I could work others out of sight
Go home change and then dance all night
Always working to provide for the family un-fussed
Providing solidarity, stability and trust
Now recalling a lifetime of heartache, laughter and tears
That has shaped my character over the years
Forever swallowing pills now to ease the tension
For the aches and pains that justify my pension
Sitting watching the World go by I can relax
I have spent a lifetime working and paying tax
Critically analysing all the changing ways
Things being done differently since earlier days
A generation altogether more open, less inhibited
With breasts and thighs forever being exhibited
Shoe laces and buttons are no longer easy
The digestive system has an aversion to things greasy
Body shrinking, shoulders rounding stature less erect
Now seriously minded my judgement more circumspect
Looking towards the closure of life`s gallery
The realisation that I am now a tail-end Charlie.

UNFORGETTABLE

In far off day`s when I was young and truly smitten
Inadequate letters to a beautiful girl were written
Destiny dictating our journey through life not a shared way
Now in the twilight zone maybe I can lighten your day
What was ,what was, that was then
Now is now, and a bit of fun with a pen
You may wonder how crazy it may be
The way you have lasted in my memory
Those qualities that I unwittingly spied
Passed me by un-acknowledged and un-recognised
 A lifetime,   a multitude of people long short and tall
Yet those memories of you linger above them all.
What are those qualities you have that are unique
That for fifty years with no one would I speak
The charm that once filled my heart with desire
Long unseen still with the power to motivate and inspire
Clouded memories of long ago, dust covered in the shadow
Like flitting butterflies in a sun kissed, flower filled meadow
Do I prefer those memories in the mind that are toyed?
Would I risk confrontation for fear of them being destroyed?
Long ago I failed, but once again I try
To keep a spring in your step and a twinkle in the eye
But sadly I have to confess for my sins
Only I know where truth ends and poetic licence begins.

THE TRUTH

That beautiful lass my first real girlfriend
Memories!   A warmth of feeling I hope will never end
Oh! Why when I have plenty of company and am well fed
Is it that memories of you still enter my head
That youthful friendship admired and adored
Like a continent visited that remained un-explored
What is the mystical power over me that you possessed
That still those fond memories linger above the rest
Would I live in hope my heart strings could again be pulled
Or risk finding time and memory has left me fooled
Born and developed in the innocence of youth
Could they withstand the realities of a lifetimes truth
For over fifty years to one another we have been unknown
Time for lifestyle changes family and other interests to be sown
Could I risk that fondness and kindness of thought
Ever being dashed and reduced to nought.

SIMPLY THE BEST

However many girls I may have kissed
You are the one the heart has forever missed
Of all the twists and turns life has had me endure
The memory of you is the most precious and pure
For me you were the one on the mountains crest
Sadly I was the one unequal to your test
The past long ago recorded and often reviewed
There is no doubt you should have been more fervently pursued
That friendship had it developed and put to the test
Could it have been simply the best.

A DINNER INVITATION

Those first loves that may never have ended
But have lain dormant for a lifetime suspended
As if locked in a deepfreeze forever preserved
An aperitif "you once prepared" still waiting to be served?

BOB KIRK`S HONEY TREE

Bob Kirk having moved into his "retirement home", a house in a 10 acre wood with ponds and lakes and decided to make it a showplace and with wife Sally`s help threw himself into gardening. After two or three years a local group of seventeen gardeners came to visit and see the developments. After showing them round most of the garden Bob announced that the tree in front of them was his "honey tree" and went and put his arms round the tree and hugged it. He then pointed out to the group the three holes that had been made by woodpeckers at some time previously and that there were bees coming and going from the top two holes and had made it their home, and that he had fixed a tube running into a jam jar he had suspended which appeared to be collecting what Bob claimed was the surplus honey from the bees nest within the tree from the bottom hole. The group noted it was an oak tree and questioned if it was a special sub species of oak Bob claimed it was and that is why it was unusual, elaborating on the virtues, With the group intrigued and one lady now hugging the tree, Bob thought it was time to reveal his hoax and admit that the honey, like liquid in the jam jar, was cold tea.

DREAMS

Dreams uninhibited or without logic in any way
Often reflecting memories of a long lost day
Events of a long gone or rarely visited scene
With people present and the past, never again to be seen
Dreams that come in light sleep and are un-co-ordinated
Yet in the morning rarely remembered or related
Forgotten memories surprisingly still lodged in the mind
Inconsequential, never recalled but rarely unkind
Perpetuated in dreams in a manner that never did exist
Jumbled thoughts and memories that may be sublime
Yet not to be recalled or remembered by breakfast time
Fragments and tit bits one never realised were in the mind
From both now and then mixed together in a rare find
The effects of times, people and places of the past
Time like the dreams to be enjoyed as long as they last
Dreams of playing and running wild on acres of land
Where now houses or factories and other buildings stand
A jumble of places unvisited and people never met
All appearing in a fantasy of a rambling un-controlled fret
Dreams of cream cakes and chocolates that are yummy-yummy
Dreams supposed to be sexier if you have slept on your tummy
Never to be remembered a dream that lasted forever more
I wonder if such hallucinations rank on the intelligence score.

PRECOCIOUS PRODIDGY

That childhood talent, unbelievable unless seen
Exceptional skills that galvanise the team
Such precocious abilities we are told
Developed, future stardom they will hold
Moving from junior to under thirteen`s
Determination and single minded ambition one gleans
Then wider interests begin to make an intrusion
Into what was once complete devotion
The wisdom of seeking success on a wider scale
Should the specialised approach be of no avail
Pleasure of life appreciated on a broader spectrum
Free of restrictions of the dedicated doctrine
Who can tell in personal terms what may be the cost
If by not reaching that pinnacle, what is lost
Could that dedication have yielded a medal?
If a broader intellect had not taken a foot off the pedal
What may have been lost in the narrow specialist field
Could create benefits , with a greater yield
Depending on whether the lust for glory is found
Or the desire for comfort and company abound
Does the nature, lust for admiration from others
Or gain contentment from benefitting brother`s
At the end of the day, to be judged a specialist legend
Or by a broader circle, as a friend
From childhood genius and precociousness
Fate will play it`s part in dictating life`s success.

OCTOBER

The Autumn sun now lower in the sky with more glare
Variable weather an altogether more changeable affair
Thoughts moving away from salads and barbecues
Towards mashed potatoes, casseroles and stews
When trees take on Autumn's most colourful range
Steadily from summer to winter it makes it's change
Time for us to think of the change to the winter sphere
Bringing thoughts of warmer clothing and rain gear
Last vestiges of summer the countryside adopting autumnal hues
Preparing us for darker days and the winter blues
Gardens and flowers enjoying their last flourish
Of brilliant colour before frosts bring their finish
Beautiful hedgerows with berries on thorn bushes and holly
The need for wellington boots, raincoats and a brolly
Autumn winds swaying the boughs on trees
Pressurising and tugging at the yellowing leaves
 Finding the winter duvet, and animals thinking of hibernation
 Most harvests completed and larders stocked in anticipation
Some days creating the need of central heating or a fire
On others wash day blues thank goodness for a tumble drier
On the roads potholes, puddles and spray
As travellers, freight and commuters make their way
Rain in October rarely enough to cause a flood
Yet sugar beet trailers and lorries cover the road in mud
When shops and roadside stalls make pumpkins their scene
Some for pies, others for a candlelit appearance on Halloween.

NOVEMBER

With little but a fire on the fifth to remember
Is, there a month as dull and dreary as November?
 Summer and Autumn days that left us upbeat
Now changed clocks and temperatures requiring heat
The time now past for shirt sleeves
Just the constant chore of raking up leaves
A month devoted to consolidation and conservation
Building for December`s great winter celebration
Autumn to winter that`s what November links
Without any of next month`s parties and high jinks
Dark winter nights with land wet under foot
With little to cheer unless on a pheasant shoot
As no shaving month November can be cheered
For promoting the growth of a moustache or a beard
Remembrance day`s poppy appeal focussing our attention
On the heroes of World wars who fought unsung
For wine lover`s it`s the time for Nouveau Beaujolais
And pomegranate month, if you live in the USA
The month celebrates its birth flower, the chrysanthemum
Awareness month for cancers, pancreatic, stomach and lung
We need to wait till November is on its way
To celebrate with the Scot`s on the Thirtieth, St Andrew day.

AUTUMN LEAVES

The time of year when green leaves turn to gold
And the warmth of summer to be replaced by cold
Changing from green to golden yellow or brown
Heralding the time soon for leaves to flutter down
Such colours when highlighted by the autumn sun
Provide a scene to cheer the hearts of everyone
The vista of beautiful colours a sight to behold
We can only observe the onset of winter to unfold
Those branches once fully leaved and green
Will once again be bare revealing views unseen
Fallen leaves raked and put in heaps to make compost
Possibly a home for a hibernating hedgehog to avoid frost
Leaves that can cause floods by blocking drains
Or falling on railway lines slowing down trains
The coating of leaves that will cover the forest floor
Has protected creatures and invertebrates for evermore
A time when birds congregate and form flocks
Winter heralded at October's end by the changing of clocks
Stores for wood burning stoves already filled with logs
In the bedroom duvets now getting higher rated togs
The autumn sun no longer so high in the sky
Creating danger as it shines in the motorists eye
Now wearing jumpers and shirts with longer sleeves
Amongst the things associated with autumn leaves.

AUTUMN

With a declining summer sun
Natures preparations for winter are begun
A steady reduction in the number of daylight hours
End to the summer's succession of colourful flowers
Gone the sight and sound of pollen foraging bees
Now that leaves are steadily falling from trees
An ever increasing risk of an overnight frost
Plants moved to greenhouse for fear they may be lost
The last Sunday in October no matter what, rain or shine
Changing the clocks the ending of British summer time
Grass growth slowed, lawn mowers work pretty well done
Soon to be serviced and waiting for spring to come
Central heating switched on is the order of the day
Very little sun with sky's that seem continually grey
Almost forgotten happy days playing on tennis courts
Concentration now focussed on indoor or winter sports
When one may say without contradiction or fear
It is both the end and beginning of the farming year
With the harvesting of sugar beet, maize and potatoes
Rape crops then winter barley and wheat planted in rows
All standing proud with their growing green shoots
If walking on fields or footpaths expect muddy boots
Time when farmers without livestock may seek leisure
For many pheasant shooting is a favourite pleasure
In places the air getting filled with different sounds
Birds from Northern climes reaching their wintering grounds
Sometimes its wind and rain that can quickly change
Consistent with our meteorological autumnal range
Temperatures rarely affecting activities out in the open air
Yet making it prudent to find some extra layers to wear
Autumn a transitional period that gets to have its say
Preceding winter which leads us to the years shortest day.

PYLONS

I Look out of my window, and what do I see
A line of pylons for electricity
Standing tall majestically carrying the power
That keeps the country going hour after hour
At the touch of a switch there is light
 On demand at any time day or night
The washing machine the cooker or to vacuum the floor
In the workshop the grinder, sander or power saw
In offices and hospitals for computers, heating and much more
Electricity is there for every mundane chore
Standing resolutely erect against all storms
Supplying the Nation's energy to be utilized in all forms
Silhouetted against the sky carrying electricity
A comfort for those with needs like me
The lifeblood of the country carried by you
Unobtrusive sentinels now part of the view.

DOUGHNUTS

Saturday mornings, that's when I think of you
After shopping, with Morrison's Doughnuts 35P for two
Time to think of all those for whom I care
And it is with you that I would choose to share
In a life, that has had many a strange twist
Raspberry jam filled doughnuts are hard to resist
At 35P for two that's one more, than I need
To eat them both, is tantamount to greed
Yes it is you that I would choose to meet
To share and indulge in my Saturday treat.
Element of surprise lost if I rang on the phone
Maybe something you, would rather not eat?
Obstacles in sharing my doughnuts with you
To hang with it, a cup of coffee, and I eat two
As I eat the doughnuts with sugar on my lips
Reading the paper and drinking my coffee in sips
I am remembering you, of whom I choose to dream
Next time it may be chocolate éclairs filled with cream.

(Huh! now the blighters have changed their prices.)

SNAIL RACING

Oh! Neil Riseborough of snail racing fame
How ever did you evoke such a stimulating game
An attraction at various functions and fetes
Snail racing boosting attendances at the gates
Oh! What is it you need to succeed?
Have you developed a special racing breed
Oh! Neil Riseborough of snail racing fame
How do you live with such an exciting game
Tell me if they are thinner are they quicker?
Than those that are squatter and thicker.
Oh! Neil Riseborough. You needed excitement and how
After deciding to sell your last cow
As the pioneer you have gained glory and fame
With the tension and excitement that is your game
Oh! Is it a foot they have to traverse?
Always forward of course never in reverse
The uninitiated never appreciate the finer points of the game
That has brought you this glory and fame
As they go faster struggling to make up time
Can you notice if it`s a thinner trail of slime
How over the time Norfolk`s Tourism has expanded
Due to snail racing almost single handed
Oh! Neil Riseborough of snail racing fame.
Thank you for giving Norfolk it`s individualistic game.

LEADER OF MEN

Oh! to prove "how I can be a leader of men"
By driving at 40 mph on the single carriage way bits of the A10
When it came to head boy or a prefect
I was never the one they chose to select
Although I thought I may have been in the bunch
Never the one picked when it came to the crunch
All through life carrying out duties to the letter
Never got the top job, there was always someone better.
Although the top job was always missed
I was the one relied upon to assist
Never to be credited for firing the gun
But for providing the bullets I was the one
For information and analysing research I was the feeder
But never the front man designated as leader
Always quietly competent, unassuming and mellow
never thought to be as charismatic as the other fellow
Whilst always recognised as the guiding hand
Yet never credited as the leader of the band
Often responsible for plotting and planning the game
Yet never, should disaster strike be the one to blame.
With all that guile and thought out gen
I could and should have been a leader of men
If it hadn`t been for nervousness and fear
I would have been the front man and not in the rear
You dominating personalities, "I will show you the way"
When you get caught up in traffic on a single carriage way
"I will show you I am a Leader of Men"
If you get behind me on the narrow stretches of the A10.

HERBIE HUCKLEBERRY

Herbert Huckleberry of Hardley Dever
Some local places he visited others never
On market days from early morn all day long
Herbie would be always in the midst of the throng
Whether produce or livestock reared on his land
He was always there to see it sold first hand
All sorts of goods whether household or farm
At auction if thought cheap he would raise an arm
A bit of general dealing like his father that was the way
Always ready to sell it on in the next town another day
His long suffering wife often heard to mutter
Not knowing how he would fill the house with clutter
The poor woman left to run the small farm all day
Whilst Herbie went on living in his individualistic way
With a few sheep, pigs, rabbits and hens
At weekends he would help to muck out the pens
Refurbish and tinker with goods he had bought cheap
Thinking about the pound or two he might reap
Repairing goods he had bought at the marts
From his shed full of unsold spare parts
With rusting screws, nuts and bolts of every size
If Herbie couldn`t find the right one it was a surprise
Damaged furniture he would bodge it if he could
With a tube of super glue and another piece of wood
How much stuff he had was hard to tell
Much of what he bought he couldn`t resell
Rarely giving anything very much thought
Hoping there would be a fortune in what he bought
Always scheming and struggling to make ends meet
And promising to take the missus on holiday for a treat
But in truth Herbie Huckleberry of Hardley Dever
Knew for a fortune he would need to be more clever.

COMMON COLD

Lethargy, aching limbs, feeling old
All symptoms of the simple common cold
The first signs a repetitive sneeze
The start of this viral infection, not a disease
Runny eyes, Phlegm, stuffiness and a headache
Two or three days regardless of the pills you take
Three days coming not that you know
Three days with you and three to go
Both business and social life impaired
Regardless of treatment and how one is cared
That running nose forever being blown
Where the infection contracted? likely never known
Bin full of used tissues on the floor
Football team playing, can't be bothered with the score
Fatigued, appetite lost, left feeling depressed
Often overwhelmed by the need for sleep and rest
The sort of infection the doctor dismisses as a virus
But not diminishing the way it tires us
The throat and voice affected becoming hoarse
As this cruel affliction takes its course
A miserable existence for a day or two to endure
With a host of helpful tips for relief, but no cure
Nasal passages and sinuses uncomfortably blocked
The medicine cabinet helpless, although well stocked
Once over it, we are immune and have resistance
If others are infected not bothered to keep our distance
But those watery aching eyes were no fun
When that continually snotty nose, was on the run.

INTERDEPENDENCE

All species interdependent that is nature`s way
Some are carnivores in the sky like birds of prey
A multitude of insects of which we are unaware
That birds like swallows feed on whilst in the air
Fauna and forage crops growing randomly every year
Providing nourishment for rabbits, hares and wild deer
There`s birds that forage with great skill
On all types of grain and seeds even road kill
Rats and mice and similar species regarded as evil
Along with invertebrates from silver fish to weevil
Nature`s ability to provide without intervention
Now helped by wild life experts with good intention
No matter whether winter, spring, summer or fall
Nature alone without help can take care of it all
Flowers of spring and summer we welcome their arrival
Pollinated by bees and insects ensuring their survival
All have their parts to play even if you don`t think twice
Whether it be snakes, lizards, snails, grubs or lice
Both among animals or plants where there is seeding
Nature has devised amazing ways of avoiding inbreeding
A marvel how nature without any scientific tools
Created mechanisms to protect individual genetic pools
Will there come a challenge nature hasn`t faced yet
If so nature will find a way to negate the biggest threat
There is no doubt plant and animal species are hard to beat
And may present challenges that humans have yet to meet
Homo sapiens for all their technology and drive
Will find nature provides the answers it needs to survive
Interdependence amongst species clearly that is nature`s way
It has ruled the World since time immemorial to this day.

INSPIRATION AND MOTIVATION

Oh! the turmoil you caused in my mind Mr John O Gleave
Is way beyond anything you are likely to believe
The levels of inspiration and motivation generated by B P
As I revert to my memory to list those inspirational to me
For painting and decorating there could be no other
Than Pete and Gwen my first wife's father and mother
t is equally true there are others who hold a shield
For skills they instilled in a different field
The turmoil you caused in my mind Mr John O Gleave
Is way beyond anything you are likely to believe
Of one who inspired and motivated me to a higher key
Was determined not to be part of my life's destiny
As through life I have tread a purposeful course
With never a thought of the past or remorse
Oh! the Turmoil you caused Mr John O Gleave
Is way beyond anything you are likely to believe
Possibilities for a future once generated
Although sadly not to be, and I was left deflated
Whilst I have worked hard nose to the ground
Never again such inspiration and motivation have I found
Oh! Mr John O Gleave it has always been plain to see
I never received the inspiration and motivation you got from BP.

RHODODENDRONS AND AZALEAS

If beautiful blooms of rhododendrons and azaleas be your quest
You will find Norfolk the home of East Anglia`s best
A plant that is a national emblem in many foreign parts
Here, in May it provides a burst of colour to warm our hearts
From the South it may be Somerleyton Hall you choose to go
Then head towards Norwich on the shrub lined road to Haddiscoe
Journey northwards past the fine city of Norwich on to the Broads
From Wroxham to Hoveton Hall and rhododendrons that strike a few
chords.

Now ever onwards for the two that really leave a mark
The great array and wonderful views in Repton`s Sheringham Park
While for some it`s a close run thing, for me Stody Lodge takes the prize
With those rhododendron and azalea gardens ten acres in size
Not only in front of the house but across the road as well
Through the woods to that enchanting vista by the lake in the dell
Sheringham and Stody are the must visits and that is my story
If you desire to see rhododendrons and azaleas in their majestic glory.

THE ROSE

Beyond any shadow of doubt the nations favourite flower
Epitomising our heraldry and nationalistic power
From time immemorial the flower of universal acclaim
From Asia and Europe across to the Americas, peace it`s declared aim.

Heralded as a symbol in festivals and celebration`s
Across the World in many varying nations
The white rose indicating the purity of light from above
The red rose the most cherished symbol of undying love.

The rose creating the peace to inspire a genius
Identifying Greek and Roman goddesses Aphrodite and Venus
A flower of such quintessential heraldic beauty
Calling true born citizen`s across nations to do their duty.

In Bulgaria for centuries it has been the peasant`s toil
To cultivate and harvest roses for the production of their oil
With such a multitude of colours to make one wonder
With varieties such as standard, tea, rambling or floribunda.

A flower always destined to be a centre piece in a floral dance
One which can never be denied for it`s beautiful fragrance
Throughout the world, a symbol on the many motif`s it adorns
It is the innocence of bushes that they have prickles not thorns.

For plant breeders and rose growers new varieties is the game
Often honouring privileged celebrities who lend their name
Each year it is advisable to manicure and prune
To ensure the roses greatest spectacle in June.

To a friend who runs in marathons

THE MARATHON

The challenge, endurance and dedication
The satisfaction that I could run a marathon
The Camaraderie and sense of fellowship
Of those destined for self-imposed hardship
The nervous excitement and tension
Of lining up and waiting for the starters gun.
Out on the road mile after mile to pound
More and more energy always needing to be found
Every mile, every step one less
Each one depleting reserves and creating stress
What at the start was a smile on the face
Has now turned into a grimace.
But mile after mile at a steady stride
Driven by confidence, ego and pride
As the last miles approach, can you endure the pain
You question whether you will ever do it again
But then the finishing line is in sight
Completing a mighty task, a feeling nothing could blight.
The respect of colleagues, friends and others you will never know
leaves a worthy reward and a personal glow
The congratulations for a race well run
The knowledge that it`s another thing well done
For me it will only be a dream
I can never be a member of your elite team.

END OF A LINE

I will not feature in future generations hereditary
For a father, that was never to be me
The pleasures of parenthood, never mine to share
Not my fortune, to have a son or daughter as an heir
Not for me holding my own baby to my chest
Providing security, ensuring it got it's rest
All the simple things that I was denied
 Never kept awake at night by a baby that cried
The smile of recognition as I came through the door
From a baby still not old enough to crawl on the floor
A love that is greater than any other
A baby the flesh and blood of a father and mother
Adjusting one's life to accommodate their needs
Nappies to be changed and frequent feeds
The marvel of the first words as they begin to talk
Putting things out of reach as they start to walk
Witnessing their own independence starting to rule
Long before the age to start going to school
The bond of fellowship that becomes ever more entwined
As parents struggle with the questions of a developing mind
Never was there a challenge to me
Of teaching a tiny tot it's ABC
Simple things that sound like a bore
Teaching a child, to hold a crayon so it can draw
Never for me to experience the joy's and tears
The unconditional love of a child in those early years
Till the time for School to take a hand
 And watch the independence develop strand by strand
School plays and extra curriculum activities to support
The youthful endeavours in the field of sport
Watching carefully as they grow to become free
But not for me, I am a cul-de- sac on the family tree.

FAMILY TREE

Oh! John Fennigworth and your family tree
Making a connection between you and me
With no apparent disputes and everything in harmony
Names making us all equal in the family tree
Nothing to indicate the go-getter from the sleeper
But all suffering the same fate at the hands of the grim reaper
Largely ignoring everybody`s heartache and tears
No record of peaks and chasms or how they toiled
Just births, marriages and deaths all unsoiled.
Oh! John Fenningworth how you have invigorated the memory
In your quest to delve into this branch of your extended family
Our heritage and ancestors something of which we had no choice
No doubt the only thing we all speak of with the same voice
A family who have sought their fortunes on many a foreign shore
Now to be found in the America`s ,the Antipodes, Asia and more
Branches of the family now far flung
Like a spreader going down a field spreading dung.
With diverse interests religions and politics unstated
United by a family tree proving we are related
Recording a family with a common thread
Each and every one with a beginning made in a bed
Now with all your pedigree data documented and collected
Although some not worthy of scrutiny and being inspected
Oh! John Fenningworth when you have finished taking stock
How many more are there unrecorded, born out of wedlock.

THE BONNIE LASS of KIRBY-LE-SOKEN

Oh that fair lass from Kirby-Le-Soken
Who in far off days left my heart broken
Of all the girls I have ever known
Were I a king, she could have shared my throne
Sparkling eyes of the girl from the house on the hill
With a smile never to be forgotten, remembered still
 Now more wily, I am past youths first flush
Recalling feminine charm that made my blood rush.
That lovely maiden from Kirby-Le-Soken
Who stole my heart, it was loves first token
 How I remember those first feelings of pride
At places and dances with that girl by my side
A lass ambitious with a sense of fun and desire
Who captured my heart and set it on fire
If I still wonder how such a beautiful flower grows
I need to go the extra mile, to Beaumont-Cum-Moze.

WALLY`S WIDOW

Wally`s widow full of pranks and fun
Carrying on with mischief he long ago begun
All good natured nothing immoral or uncouth
The spirit embraced by many in a long departed youth
All kinds of tricks played and practical jokes
On her married girlfriends and their blokes
Maybe from her pocket a joke spider may appear
To create mirth when the unwary registered fear
She always regarded it as great fun
To pour you a cup of tea when the saucer was joined as one
If in your house a likely trick with look-alike dog poo
To make you think your pet had done a number two
If in her house beware if she passed behind your chair
She may appear with scissors in hand and a lock of hair
With so much fun and laughter in her heart
Always a whoopee cushion for the sound of a fart
With some thoughts rather less pure
Usually stink bombs smelling of manure
Hardly a trick missed she was into the lot
If she saw you writing it would be the artificial ink blot
Wally`s widow always smiling and of ample girth
Forever trying to keep the street alive with mirth
Wally tried and Wally died, no longer here
Her feelings masked by the superficial and insincere.

HORRY LEES

Late home from work came Horry Lees
His life spent in the woods lopping trees
He had stopped at the pub for a beer
Pending his pay, he was full of dread and fear
Yet not uncommon for Horry to be skint
As he entered, with a lopsided grin and a squint
Horry's earnings were never too good
Wife Elsie always careful with food.
Her long running battle with a shortage of cash
Meant a common menu was sausage and mash
Forever counting the pennies in her change
To purchase foods in the cheapest range
 Very rare for them to have a Sunday roast
More often making do with beans on toast.
Now for many years it has been reported
Horry's home-life has been somewhat distorted
His wife always in fear of what she would have to lose
If Horry stopped at the pub for a bender on the booze
Elsie's living room carpet and curtains now faded
Typical of household responsibilities Horry evaded
Married life now a pre-determined hostile co-existence
Either one taking care to keep the other at a distance
Wife sleeping in a separate room to avoid his snore
Horry, with a rattle louder than any chainsaw.

Two verses, to a friend in the depth of despair after the loss of her husband

CAROL

Oh! please do not despair
Carol so bonny and fair
While the future is not ours to see
Believe in how much brighter it can be
With new friends and challenges to meet
New opportunities, ventures and places to greet.
Oh! Carol so bonny and fair
The lass with golden hair
That has tints of autumn gold
You have many talents and abilities untold
To hang with a humdrum existence
Reach out for enjoyment with determined persistence.
Oh! Carol so bonny and fair
Your personality has a special air
Oh! Carol never forget what's gone before
It's made you what new friends will adore
The past should be remembered with sincerity
A foundation for future happiness and prosperity.

THE SMILE

Oh! Carol with the winning smile
The Carol so plagued by adversity
With the passing of time and that winning smile
Have no fear you will move on to lasting security
Ahead lies a life of friendship and laughter
A life no longer dogged with frustration
A few months or maybe a year, then the peace you are after
Although for a while your road will be rocky without elation.
Oh! Carol with the winning smile
Don`t underestimate the strength of friendship and concern
Of the friends and Acquaintances who you have known awhile
They are there to try and help you find the life you yearn
Whilst encouraging and admiring your dignity and decorum
You will have to reach out for new horizons, with style.

SCRAPHEAP CHALLENGE

Oh! Yvonne how will you manage
As you face your scrapheap challenge
To be told it is the end of the line
When you are a fit spritely sixty nine
 We all know one thing for certain
Nobody ever stitched a better curtain
Harrods, Selfridges and fine establishments
Where only the best left customers content
Took for granted your undoubted skill
And never quibbled about paying the bill
Sadly though as you have grown older
There has been irritation and a troublesome shoulder
Now with hard times it`s the bosses sad tale
To say "Yvonne it`s time to draw the veil"
With the future looking so uncertain
"It is with regret we draw the final curtain."
You would need to be blind not to see
Adjustments will be made to recognise the finality
To hang with needles, scissor`s and tape measure
Time to think of freedom and leisure
They say if you just work life is a bitch
Welcome to happiness, having sown your last stitch
In the morning if you oversleep it`s not a disaster
The morning alarm clock is no longer the master
Time to relax and cultivate interests of your taste
 Whether old or new without undue haste
No longer orders and deadlines to meet
Leisurely looking in shops as you go down the street
Restriction`s removed time of opportunity and bold decisions
Chance for adventure and time to create new visions.

GOOD MORNING

When the clock reaches the significant number
A ringing bell shakes us out of our slumber
The shrill tone of that designated alarm
Controlled by the involuntary movement of a sleepy arm
Temptation to roll over and stay out of view
The idea soon abandoned by the need of the loo
Aware of the day`s challenges we should not shirk
Our lifestyles financed by our hours of work
Taking care not to linger too long with the toothpaste
Towards another day of dread, credibility or hope
Destined to begin with water and soap
As every day begins and starts its own story
 Whether summer sunshine or a winter`s frost that`s hoary
Electricity demands increasing dramatically by the hour
As business gets going, kettles and toaster`s compete for power.

BIG BARNEY O-TOOLE

Here`s to big Barney O-Toole
Bumptious and Belligerent but nobody`s fool
 With hands on control over his very large farm
Yet compassionate, seeing smaller neighbours take no harm
 Looking out from the house to pastures with quality cattle and sheep
To the other side, regimented fields of barley and wheat
Fiercely proud of his inheritance and the family`s rural roots
A champion of hunting, fishing, shooting and all country pursuits
Always keen on sports especially rugby and hockey
Tried point to pointing once, but too big to be a jockey
Never a football fan his school didn`t have a team
Regarding it a sport for people with a lower esteem.
With a manner that could sometimes strike fear
An asset when staff or parish councillors needed to jump into gear
With positive opinions on all subjects he can talk for evermore
At the Country Landowners, the NFU and committee`s galore
Discussing the problems of the day in an effort to find a solution
Satisfied that his benevolence has made a worth wile contribution
Always convinced he deserved life`s rich bounty
To be accepted into the highest social circle in the county
It has never occurred to him in his wildest dream
That anyone would question him not matching his own self esteem
Family and friends say his bark is worse than his bite
Soft and ineffectual as a puppy dog if other people are out of sight.

BIRTHDAY

Each year on your birthday It is my sincere intent
Too you a valued friend I express a personal sentiment
Oh! How meaningfully I search for words to define my view
Sentences that reflect the high regard I have of you
Your birthday approaches and I can`t think of a verse
The minds gone blank, it must be writers curse
I am looking for words of just the right tone
That are attributable to you and you alone
A phrase that is definitive accurate and personal
That truly reflects on you a deserving individual
I wish I could think of words in a mixture and blend
Of a worthy content to congratulate you my friend
How I sit and think watching the passing of time
But darned if I can come up with a decent rhyme
How sad that I sit here nonplussed and bleating
Unable to find words adequate for your greeting
I can do no more than in a very ordinary way
Write.

KEITH: ENJOY A HAPPY BIRTHDAY.

YOUTHFUL DAYS

The fondest memories that have lingered in the mind
A legacy of far off days that were carefree and kind
Days blessed with the freedom and energy of youth
Life blessed with pleasure, removed from the harsh truth
New found unrestricted freedom being put to the test
Regardless of whether parental advice may have been best
Assured yet still uncertain, relying on guidance when needed
With that parental advice often going unheeded
Ambitious ideas, but not bearing responsibility that mattered
Too early for those youthful dreams to be shattered
Early faltering footsteps into the adult world, ours to explore
New experiences and visiting places we had never been before
New ventures and activities appealing some at prohibitive cost
Some adopted others losing their attraction, interest lost
A world with so many diverse interests impossible to explore
Day to day life restricting the opportunity to open many a door
A world where many interests and aspirations have gone untried
Where through time, and other preoccupations motivation has died
Youthful energy stimulating the desire to impress
In a life of freedom and protection that`s free of stress
In a great social merry go round with little time to rest
Developing friendships, a lifetime companion the unstated quest.

On old age when capabilities can fail to meet either expectations or possibilities

SEVENTY FIVE YEARS YOUNG

Oh! How we react to the passing of the years
Moving at a more relaxed pace in lower gears
A lifetime spent learning how to duck and dive
At work and marriage till reaching seventy five
Years that passed quickly looking back seem an eternity
Achieving the lifetime award of watching television free!
Time now to sit and review times past and relax
State pension provided, but paid for and more with tax.
The multitude of changes we have seen
Things so much different to what they had been
Darned socks patched trousers and jumpers granny would knit
Passed down, usually too big or small, rarely did they fit
Life dominated by work with few treats or kicks
Lucky to get a cuddle with a girl in the back row at the flicks
Long gone, Teddy Boys, Mod`s and Rocker`s on scooters
Now it`s mobile phones with TV`s i pads calculators and computers
Horses all gone tractors with hydraulics providing the power
When wages were not much more than four or five bob an hour
Now farming with modern technology to the fore
One man with big machines a thousand acres or more.
But then Roger Bannister made everybody smile
With the help of Brasher and Chataway he ran a four minute mile
1966 the world Cup staged and won, a nation fit to burst
Led by Alf Ramsey and Bobby Moore with goals by Geoff Hurst
Our parents rubbish was carelessly thrown
Now Valued Antiques, if only we had known
With a host of memories locked in our brain-box
Even though sometimes it is a struggle to undo the locks.

More than a dozen Prime Ministers too numerous to mention
All no doubt determined to serve with honest intention
Believing at the time they were best placed to lead the nation
Yet never one of them finding the way to conquer inflation
Ted Heath with the Common Market and a three day week
Miner`s on strike, Arthur Scargill, did continually shriek
Maggie Thatcher was not for turning and was a long time there
But lived to see she was not outdone by Blair
Gone were the days of rationing of food
When McMillan went on about never having it so good.
Chinese and Indian take-ways arriving to savour our lips
 No longer just restricted to fish and chips
Little Chef roadside restaurants started a trend
Now it appears their race has come to its end
McDonalds along with Burger King needed to be tried
Not to mention Pizza Hut and Kentucky Fried
TV cooks Zena Skinner, Philip Harben and Fanny Craddock a myth
Now a plethora recently dominated by Jamie Oliver and Deila Smith
Now with pressure on everything having to be done in a hurry
No longer Sunday Roast, we are told the national dish is "Curry".
Hard working, regarding state handouts as abhorrent
Benefit scroungers described in an undisguised torrent
Our endeavours have not entirely been in vain
Recognising values the current generation struggles to maintain
Yes sadly as Senior Citizens we are getting old
But our memories are as rich as a pot of gold
Oh to hang with it our contribution is not done
We are just more relaxed and we still enjoy a bit of fun.

REMEMBERING

The unfettered memories of the freedom of youth
 Now a complex mixture of fantasy and truth
Recalled now in twilight years at leisure
Of things making, early faltering footsteps a pleasure
People, events, anecdotes, remembered that are cherished
Others less worthy, insignificant events may have perished
None of us knowing how life would put us to the test
Doing what we thought right at the time, as best
Those precious memories of which one may often think
That may be recalled by an unapparent connected link
Years spent yearning, earning and learning
With differing circumstances always changing and turning
Thoughts scrolling back over the years
Recalling anecdotes of happiness heartache and tears
Revealing both ugliness and kindness that have been shown
 Both from and to us by people we have known
The mind with a lifetime of clutter running free
Reminding ourselves of the inner self others seldom see
Those inner secrets and thoughts, a lifetime concealed
Recalled remembered but unlikely ever to be revealed.

LIFE

Always told there is not much between the ears
But here I am, I have reached the twilight years
Still able to remember what was and when
A pleasure now to recall and record with a pen
Early school days during the war it was begun
The years of exploring woods and fields having fun
School days when early friends were made
Lessons learned and various sports played
Going out to youth clubs and Saturday night dances
Lots of beautiful girls with smiles and glances
The search of a lifelong partner the unstated quest
With all the fun of finding out which may suit best
Then the focus of work and getting married
Realising all the responsibilities you now carried
Before you knew it a family, your own brood
More and more work to provide them with food
With years quickly passing and then they are flown
 Now just the two of us Darby and Joan
Time for fun and travel without a care
Only to find you are number one babysitters. Not fair
Lucky with health not really much more than a few chills
Now a highlight going to the doctor`s for a box of pills
Suddenly it seems the stairs are getting steeper
And a cord round your neck with a radio controlled bleeper.

UNDER ACHIEVER

Looking back an under achiever that's me
 Making the most of my talents was never to be
Circumstances and excuses could be piled high
Under achieved? Lack of confidence that's why
If only I had had more courage to match my pride
I would have overcome my desire to hide
My work ethic and endeavours were matched by few
My achievements for others brought their due
I don't deny I have always enjoyed life and had fun
And those who benefited appreciated what I had done
Oh! Had I been more self-motivated I would have achieved more
Although what I did for other's was never a chore
Friends and acquaintances, the respect I have gained
Represent a wealth money would never have acclaimed
How I wonder if I had chosen another road
Stuck my neck out and carried a heavier load
 Would life have been just one unending chore
Or could I have ended up on some sunlit shore
Was my life determined by destiny
That an under-achiever, I was always to be.

THE RIVER OF LIFE

Just as with us, a river starts as a little titch
A spring feeding a pond that overflows into a ditch
From small beginnings meandering through the countryside
As it goes, joined by others getting evermore wide
Sometimes reduced to just a trickle the banks just mud
At others overflowing, the water a raging flood
Places where the banks are preserved as nature has ordained
Others where corrosion requires attention to keep them maintained
Sometimes deeper or more shallow on its own accord
Occasionally conditions allowing humans to have created a ford
Sometimes draining, at others irrigating for crops to grow
Are it`s essential duties and it`s need to flow.
Under the bridge of life the river continually flows
As in youth on towards a destination no one knows
Twists and bends sometimes more turbulent and less still
Where in past times would be the setting for a mill
At times so calm and peaceful as if over seen by a fairy
At others the angry torrents making it altogether more scary
Whether in raging torrents or when calm without urgency
Under life`s bridge water flows onwards towards the estuary
Not always flowing freely, with debris it will stutter
Just like the human mind, progress hindered by clutter.
But those gentle waves and never ending consistency
Flowing through water meadows on its way to the sea
Birds and animals finding the banks, meet their every need
Spending a lifetime where they can feed and breed
Stretch`s for fishing, boating or other pursuits of leisure
Folks wandering gaining memories they will treasure
That little river that started out as a sleeper
Now a great expanse of water wider and deeper
No longer the provider and servant of the countryside
It`s identity lost, now absorbed by the ocean`s tide.

DREAMS and PROMISES

Dreams and Promises of every kind
Designed to stimulate and tempt the mind
Offers at Christmas, Easter and bank holidays, it`s plain to see
Everybody needs either a new bed or a settee
Yes! Hurry not a moment to delay
Free credit and up to four years to pay
If a man, just saturate your body with Lynx
And be swarmed with girls ready for high jinks
Its roses and chocolates in a more subtle theme
Generating rewards in the more cultured domestic scene
Yes it`s dreams and promises on which life depends
To provide the compulsion to see what is round the bend
The driving force that makes a business expand
Or a young man seek his fortune in a foreign land.
The dream and promise of winning the lottery, Money galore
Enjoying forever, luxurious living on a sun kissed shore
No need of caution or thoughts of bills to pay
Just eat drink and be merry and live for the day
Your attendance guaranteed at all events, of any note
Without thought of the cost of any dress or coatDreams and
promises the motive for athletes striving for Olympic gold
And the everlasting fame that will be theirs to hold
Whilst a multitude of dreams and promises abound
With health and contentment dreams and promises are already found.

DESTINY

Am I what I may be, or made to be?
By some predetermined fate of destiny
Could greater or less achievements been my forte
If I had been led to decisions that pointed a different way
It is said life's fortunes are waiting to be won
But reserved for those with determination and aggression
The idea that with concentrated effort everyone wins is a fable
To have success or failure there's always those more or less able
Oh! Where is there guidance forthright and clear
 To direct us all to our most accomplished sphere.
How many among us that play a worth wile part
Can claim a satisfaction and passion in our heart
 Our schools, schoolmates, partners and friends
All directing needs and interests towards their ultimate ends
 Could it be destiny that provides some with wealth
Or does destiny predetermine ones health
 Is it destiny to be in a life changing accident
Or a humdrum life unexciting but yet content
 Fortunate are those whose life's if controlled by destiny
Enjoy good health and avoid physical adversity.

BERTIE BAKER FROM BROCKDISH

Bertie Baker from Brockdish, a Waveney lad born and bred
Muddled through life, with hardly a serious thought in his head
Fished in the river and surrounding ponds and brooks
With a hazel stick a thread and pins bent for hooks
Bertie shared an affinity with the river birds, ducks, moorhens and coots
Traversing the river banks and ponds with his forever mucky boots
Not a yard from Hoxne to Needham he didn`t know
Every twist and bend he knew how the current would flow
Often loitering around Syleham where the waters are seldom still
Waiting for his mother and sister who worked at the mill
Never an academic the teachers always found him remote
But always new more than the others about a weasel or stoat
Labelled the school dunce, unlikely to get a job with much pay
Trouble was they didn`t know much about dyslexia in his day
Always rebuffed by the girls, he suffered little or no lust
Although he seemed to favour those with a substantial bust
Got a job away from home once, working with pigs
Into his bedroom with those mucky boots, got kicked out of his digs
Wildlife on the banks of the Waveney and its surrounds his interest
Knew where swans, geese and all other sorts of birds would nest
Could tell you where frogs were most likely to spawn
Knew where to look for a kingfisher in the early morn
With his mother and sister to see he was well fed
Bertie Baker from Brockdish a Waveney lad born and bred.

Mr GONNERDU

Everything always under control nothing much to do
All problems easily solved in the mind of Mr Gonnerdu
In the garden or house that needs attention, says his wife
Gonnerdu says I`ll do it sometime so don`t go causing strife
Conifer hedge will easily be trimmed in his mind's eye
Seems unaware the darned thing is ten foot high
Hasn`t noticed that his wife`s heart bleeds
Because the driveway to the house is covered in weeds
No need to worry in his own time he will sort it alone
And refutes the suggestion it would benefit from more stone
Not his job you are sure to hear him mutter
If you suggest he goes round the house to clean the gutter
Always reckons he is prepared to roll up his sleeves
That he will go out sometime, and rake up the leaves
Tells you the last thing he will do is abandon ship
Even though he has to defer some duties with a dodgy hip
Yes of course you can rely on Mr Gonnerdu
He will tell you the jobs left undone are very few
Actually the list is about one hundred and one
Of all the jobs Mr Gonnerdu, has`nt got done
Mr Gonnerdu long since decided to just watch things pass
When he got someone else to come and cut his grass
So you can be assured despite his pledge
He will wait for someone, to come and cut his hedge
There is not a single job either inside or outside his door
That Mr Gonnerdu won`t delay and put off for evermore.

MEMORIES STORED

Aged memories now coloured and enhanced
Of long ago days when we ran, played and danced
Memories revealing forgotten secrets there to find
For years untouched in hidden corners of the mind
Minor snippets and glimpses of the past one can recall
A rich reward in secret corners that you can trawl
Of family and meaningful friends of whom we were fond
Drunken Freddie Bakeman riding his bike into the pond
The mind where anecdotes and events are stored
Laying undisturbed until something touches a cord.

The mind a bewildering gallery of many past scenes
Recording our lives, might or might not have beens
Recalling blackouts, bombs and doodle bugs in the war
Playing endlessly with simple toys, sitting on the floor
School friends some remaining unseen, now just names
Those with scholastic abilities others excelling at games
The sweet innocence of that first love in youth
As new to a youngster as cutting their first tooth
A friendship so chaste, pristine and pure
Creating memories beautiful to endure.

TURBULENT LIFE

Day`s long gone of cuddle and hold
All that remains is hatred and cold
Forthright Views and tempers flared
With Hindsight the blame equally shared
Positive opinions and stances uncompromising
Without consideration for the others feeling
Arguments based on judgements unbalanced and unfair
Two people at loggerheads not working as a pair
Grievances prolonged and so firmly entrenched
To retract our positions we lacked the strength
Aggression and arguments that continually flared
Where peace and co-operation should have been shared
Trials and tribulations with heartache coldly worn
Where companionship and affection were long since shorn
Neither one prepared to admit they could be wrong
Not attempting to even sing a verse of the others song
How freedom is relished from that fiery blast
Now that colours are no longer tied to the same mast.

WIVES

To you ladies in my life
I am sorry to have caused you so much strife
Two marriages now both ceased
All because of my love of a bovine beast
I know I should not have neglected you, "And how"
All for the love of a Holstein cow
The way the mind works is often a riddle
Unfair if you have to play second fiddle
Can I blame you, if it`s me you chose to exclude
It`s my just desserts to live my life in solitud3.

Poignant?   Or Tongue in the cheek?
Answers on a postcard next week.

Two wives, both with considerable merits in different spheres
Would I still have been married with a bit more between my ears?

A CRONE

A drone of a Crone living alone
Curtains always drawn living in the dark
A fear, Sun would blemish and leave a mark
Said to be not too fussy or worried by dirt
Never to be seen not wearing a tweed skirt
No need for clothes to be clean
No telling where the cats may have been
Benefits and Doctors prescription`s by the score
Surprised if an official gets through the door.
Like so many living alone
She must make full use of the telephone
If it`s local news, she doesn`t miss a thing
Always several questions, should she give you a ring
Should you be unwary and express your views
Be sure it will be forwarded to others as news
News of your neighbours, should you wish to learn it
You could do no better, than phone the so called hermit
A drone of a Crone living alone.

COWS

Cows lying comfortably in cubicles filled with sand
No longer grazing meadows and parkland
 Milkers standing in pits with a fan giving a cool breeze
Gone are the days of milking stools and hunched knees
Herds continue to expand and cow numbers increase
Now milking twenty or thirty a time with quick release
No more laborious cleaning with a hand brush
With high pressure water it`s done in one flush
Big tractors and mixer wagons for the feeding
Collars and computers used to control the breeding
Regular vet days to maintain herd health
And to ensure farmers, don`t accumulate any wealth
But still no time to relax you must
Your life is spent having to manage slurry.

TWO BIRDS

Two birds seen from the window make my day
As they search for food in their own way
It is unfair to ask which I like most
The stationary figure of Ollie Owl on the gate post
Or Hobby Hawk sitting on top of the telegraph pole
 Eyes searching the earth for mice, shrews or a vole
Vantage points from where they observe and survey
Constantly watching for food sources to come their way
 Ollie Owl flying effortlessly in his inimitable way
Always on the lookout for similar prey
Both achieving their objective without undue force
Swooping silently to pinion their victim with their claws
Both birds blessed with extraordinary eyesight
With Ollie Owl`s excelling at dawn or dusk in poor light
Although with his nocturnal hunting based on sound
 Making life difficult for victims on the ground
High in the sky the Hobby Hawk stationary will hover
 Looking for anything sensing danger running for cover
 Ollie Owl flying low, with a graceful glide
Ready to pounce on prey before it can hide
From above they swoop dropping like a stone
With techniques that are theirs and theirs alone.

OLD AGE

Growing older getting more ills
Mustn`t forget where I put that box of pills
Now that the digestive system is less robust
A packet of indigestion tablets are a must
Have to wear glasses the eyes are going to pot
Without my hearing aid I can`t hear a lot
Bending and twisting now somewhat restricted
I suppose arthritis was always predicted
Slow to respond, Movements not very quick
Stiffening joints maybe the blood is not so thick
Exercising no longer so pleasing
End up coughing spluttering and wheezing
Things taking longer, can`t do them at speed
Just small portions to eat used to be a good feed
Unable to undo a jar, I am losing my grip
Modern day packaging in plastic I can`t rip
Doctor`s insistent I am protected for flu
But lucky, to still be able to sit in the queue.

NOSTALGIA

Now and then when nostalgia takes a grip
Off I go romancing on a Tendring Hundred trip
The towns and villages where I once did roam
Now viewed with affinity but no longer my home
Whilst progress and developments are altering the face
Even with years of exile I am still not out of place
Re-calling adventures in Riddles and Martins woods again
Views past the farm to the Brickyards and beyond
Looking out across the fields towards the Bentley pond.
 Into St Osyth with little chance of an acquaintance to meet
As I cast a wary eye on the Priory on goings, and Mill Street
Towards Clacton with houses now forever more
Complete with a wind farm offshore
With other changes attracting my gaze
Through Kirby to Frinton and onto the Naze
Stopping on Clacton or Frinton front where ever I might be
Whether sitting in the car or walking, a stirred memory
Remembering the innocence possessed in far off days
Before the clouds and storms of life changed my ways.
The coast road from Walton to Harwich with little sight of the sea
 Along the banks of the Stour through Bradfield to Manningtree
Into rural areas but not out in the sticks
Epitomised by the farming land around Horsley Cross and Wix
From Bromley to Brightlingsea, no matter where I go
There is a cupful of memories that overflow
Of those times and people now lost forever in a misty past
Which at the time it seemed would forever last
The Tendring Hundred an evolving ever changing scene
Symbolized by the heritage and preservation of Gt Bentley Green.

THE GARDEN SHED

For all married men, including Jeff Lloyd of Welsh Border fame
The humble garden shed where men run to escape blame
The garden shed a place of peace and tranquillity
Where a man may be busy or not, without feeling guilty
The one man's right that should always be sacred
The sanctuary he finds in his garden shed
 Some men banished there by not their own choice
Others to escape from a persistent nagging voice
Free from the hatred of a wife's eyes glaring
As he practices DIY skills with a radio blaring
If necessary equipped with armchair, heater a fridge and TV
That special domain, designed for only his privacy
Where a man can work with a plane a grinder or power saw
With no need to worry about shavings on the floor
A place where all equipment is singly manned
A restricted area from which women are banned
Where the subject of domesticity can never be debated
And the needs of a woman are patently understated
Where a man's sanity can be preserved alone
If contact is needed, let it be on the mobile phone
Should a wife wish to visit, to avoid disappointment
She is wise to make a pre-arranged appointment.
Garden tools, fork, spade, rake and hoe
All lined up for easy access in a row
Hedge cutter, strimmer and lawn mower set apart
Fully maintained and always ready to start
Tools of all sorts carefully hung on racks
Boxes of screws and nails, from the largest down to tacks
A place where a multitude of past relics are stored
Many never to be used, forgotten, hidden and ignored
A Garden shed, for relaxation rather than toil

A man`s shed is secure and selfishly preserved
The wife`s solitude indoors, often undeserved
But a man in his shed is never lost
It`s his environment, where he will not be bossed.

FRENZE RIVER

How pleasant the winding banks of the Frenze
Green pastures and wild flowers blooming there
With an array of birdlife and a vista that never ends
A place to visit and spend time with never a care
Where woodlands and pylons dominate the sky
Towards Scotland wood the chance to see a Heron or a Deer
Watching Dragonflies, Bunting`s and Lark`s time soon goes by
The Cattle, Rabbits and Crows in the trees showing no fear.
The Bridges and Ford behind the Hall
Are places to relax and contemplate
And watch as autumn leaves fall
Seeing them carried downstream by the flow
As the river twists and turns past Rabbit Meadow
On by the industry of Desira and East Coast Grain
To join the Waveney`s gentle scenic flow
And in full force be part of the mighty flood plain.

DISS

As a centre of population Diss can proudly boast
Twenty miles from Norwich, Ipswich, Bury and the coast
 A place where independent Butcher`s and Baker`s still thrive
Part of the foundation that keeps historic traditions alive
At the top of the town the Church dominates with its presence
The big four banks confirming the towns importance
With an expanse of water wide and clear
The town's most notable feature the Mere
The Mere`s mouth a place to stand still
And look across to the Park and the houses on Denmark Hill
Or a place to feed the ducks and watch them swim
At Dusk a View enhanced by the lights on the Northern rim.
On Friday`s market day when country folk meet
At the Sale Ground, Market place and Mere Street
From the surrounding villages it is just a short hop
To Diss Supermarket`s for the weekly grocery shop
To find a gift less usual you don`t have to try to hard
With other shops in both Wills and Cobbs yard
There`s St Nicholas Street, named to confuse the unwary
For the Church at the bottom is that of the Virgin St Mary
For visitor`s wishing to find a bed
There`s Guest Houses the Park Hotel and the Saracens Head.
Over the years the home of many families of note
Such as Manning`s, Taylor`s and John Skelton the poet
Since 1857 in farming, TW Gaze has played it`s part
More widely recognised now for antiques and fine art
With the granting of an Hour`s parking free
Time for a dash to the shops or the Doctor`s surgery
With ever increasing developments down by East Coast Grain
For business or pleasure, London, an Hour and a half by train.

MOLES

Oh! you moles, how you are troublesome hounds
Turning my garden into hills and mounds
Now that you have strayed from the farmers land
To the few square yards I have in hand
I know tunnelling for earthworms for you is a necessary chore
But you are making maintenance of my grass patch a bore
 A creature of interest, I know your tunnels go one way round
In your network of passages and highways underground
Preferring not to meet another mole face to face
As you travel to catch worms in your workplace
Who would have guessed you would have a one way road
When you can`t read or write a highway code.
When you are active you catch more worms than you need
And store them in an underground larder for times of need
It`s been reported over a thousand have been found
In those storage larders you have created underground
Apparently paralysed with their activity suppressed
 By a toxin which you have inherently possessed
It is said you have a cavernous house set in dry soil
Under a tree or hedgerow where humans are unlikely to toil
And don`t have to give two hoot`s
Because you are three feet down underneath the roots.
I am told the molehills and runs I see
Are twenty or more yards from where your house is likely to be
The male is called a boar, a female a sow and a group a "labour"
That being said, for me you are a poor neighbour
A mole catcher should that be my urge
To catch you my persistent scourge
In years gone by when living was thin
There were fur traders with a price on your skin
Even today there are skilled hunter`s with a price on your head

I am told £40 a time when you are dead
In this land it is plain, you moles are having fun
Perhaps I should move to Ireland where there are none.

*I am indebted to my friend Mike Goddard for a lot of information
on moles, the cost of damage to feeding stuff and silage making
equipment being his concern. Not the foreign office kind, Mike
would not wish to escalate knowledge of any foreign affairs to any
higher level than they may already be.*

*I am indebted to my friend Sally Puxted, for this contribution after
she read the previous piece on moles, Sally knows far more than
I do about the creatures having studied them and has a part time
occupation catching them in the south of Kent.*

TO GARDENERS FROM THE LITTLE GENTLEMEN IN BLACK VELVET

You`ve got to see my point of view-
Don`t harm me, and I won`t harm you;
Trample my tunnels and spread my hills
That`ll be the start of ills!
Just because you live above,
 Gives you no right to poke and shove:
Though you are high, and I am lower,
I`ve still got the power to bust your mower.
Put down new turf and roll it flat-
 Irrigate- make a green mat:
For one whole day, it`ll look just fine,
But underneath, it is all mine!!
Your lawn gives me worms galore,
And every rainfall just brings more-
And when I`m full (three times a day)
I go to rest wherever I may.
Just like old Adam I like a dry bed,
Or somewhere quiet to lay my head.
Then, hungry again off go I
Searching with my vibrissae. (That`s hairs to you)
So please resist that burning urge
For broken glass down in the verge,
Wind chimes too have no effect-
Live and let live, or simply let!
No oil-soaked rags, or dodgy smells
Or other stuff some weird bloke sells
Will put me off from digging through
The plot of land that`s owned by you.
And finally I have to say
That every mole must have his day,

And when you`ve done your worst to me...
My mates will fill the vacancy!!

Written by Sally Puxted

PASSING TIME

Memories are the thing on which passing time plays
And are often coloured by the suns golden rays
Memories that are shrouded by a long gone mythological mist
Have the ability to make the mind dance and twist
Memories which over time have got enamoured
Where even wars and the hardest times become glamoured
In memories there is little that does not take on a different hue
Rainy days seldom remembered, only skies that were blue
A family member with whom it was difficult to get along
Yet the passage of time leaves a more endearing song
Battles past that were won by sheer determination and grist
Now accorded by historians with a tactical genius twist
 The mystery of the mind clouded by the passage of time
Often leaving memories evermore beautiful and sublime.

GOD'S WAITING ROOM

No longer working, free of stress and tension
The Chancellor of the exchequer is paying your pension
Now you are an OAP, and retired
The desire for work of any kind has expired
Now life no longer holds challenges, and *vroom*
Happy to sit, awaiting your turn in God`s waiting room
No need to be up at the crack of dawn
You can`t be bothered to cut the lawn
With no urgency to cause you sorrow
Don`t care whether you even do it tomorrow
With the expertise to tell others how to do a job
Whilst sitting around becoming an idle slob
A friend and neighbour, a pleasure to meet
Your lawn and garden, the "worst in the street"
You may have discomfort in your hip and be lame
But it`s plain to other`s your excuses are tame
Couldn`t care less what others think you should do
Quite content just sitting, waiting in God`s queue
In your younger days, a hard working "bod"
Now happily sitting around, a lazy old "sod"
Another drab day gone another day past
I wonder how many more before it`s your last
Happy with inactive contentment un-fussed
Regardless if the treatment of others is unjust
Now my friend I will not tell you a lie
You silly old devil, just sitting around waiting to die.

THE LAIRD AND THE LADY

The Laird was in the kitchen eating bread and honey
The lady was in the parlour counting their money
The Laird said he would put diesel in his truck and be ready to go
Hang on said the Lady I will see if we have enough dough
The Laird said the heating`s been on, I will see if the oil tank needs a fill
Wait a minute said the Lady let`s check we can pay the bill
The Laird said they were invited to a Saturday night bash
Blow that said the lady I will stop at home and save the cash
The Laird said he might not go alone, in case he got lost
At least the Lady said that would save the cost
The Laird was invited out with a friend for the day
Before you go the Lady said find out what you will have to pay
The Lairds brother liked to spend and to be posh
Better like us the Lady said, and have some Dosh
The laird said he had put on weight, Xmas not as good as it sounds
The Lady said we will go on a diet and save Pounds (£s)
The Lady said the lino is torn on the kitchen floor
The Laird said "it`s alright, it will last another 10 years or more".

VINTAGE TRACTORS

Standard Fordson on rubbers now, used to be spade lugs
A beggar to start, kept cleaning the plugs
About the farm yard and hard to beat, a Ferguson 20 TE
For hoeing beet much preferred was the Alis Chalmers B
Remember the twin seat on the David Brown
Could beat the lot for a ride into town
Still prominent today, the one they had to fear
The universally popular John Deere
The one for me that was an if and a but
That twin cylinder Field Marshall putt, putt, putt
With some others it was a competitive race
There were challenges from both Farmall and Case
And the International, Ron and Sut Lord had one
"Contractor's". They used it on their threshing drum
Sadly with modern day tractors I am completely lost
Can't understand the technology, let alone the cost.

FURRINER IN NORFOLK

IT was back in nineteen seventy three
That an Essex man in Norfolk, I chose to be
With time to appreciate the scenic beauty
Growing, adjusting to the Norfolk character
Cultivating and developing things that matter
The length and breadth I did roam
Of the county I have long since called home
Now absorbed in the culture of the county
 Being rewarded by Norfolk`s rich bounty
In the Seventies what were planted as shoots
Have grown and developed into true Norfolk roots
Now with a bond as strong as an oak tree
A Norfolk man from Essex that`s Me.

COUNTRY ROADSTERS

Country roads that seem never to end
Not long straight and bend after bend
Cottages not long ago dilapidated and to be deplored
Now very few that are not tastefully restored
Once houses for farm workers and other country fellas
Now homes for educated, new breed country dwellers
Owners welcoming the solitude of their country retreat
Free from the noise and twitching curtains of a suburban street
Now with a good sized garden of which they are proud
With the freedom if they wish to sing or shout aloud
You are welcomed to your new place to dwell
Noted you miss street lights and complain about any country smell
Integrated and accepted back into our peaceful rural days
It`s good, benefitting our local economies in so many ways
Often taking interest in wildlife, flower and fauna and asking why
On many things us native country folk may have passed by
Many more country yokels developing interest in culture and art
It is now on country roads that town and country meet
With so many town dwellers escaping from that urban street
Businesses once confined to towns can now be run from home
To be found by customers in cars with freedom to roam
The end of the war, a baby boom and soon affluence was begun
Now more than ever town and country are growing as one
So now our country dialects have a narrow range.
We know things never stay the same and expect change

WEATHER

How fortunate here in East Anglia, wc arc usually blessed
Often rained out before reaching us having started in the West
Modern satellites, weather stations and aircraft pilots reporting
Complicated logarithms and equations in computerised forecasting
Local and National forecasts after the news on BBC and ITV
Surprisingly how often their predictions don`t quite agree
Forecasts to your individual post code is now possible they claim
Sadly sometimes not much better than a novice darts players aim
Summer heat wave predicted temperatures of thirty degrees or more
An almighty rush to the beaches, sales of sun cream soar
Thunder and lightning possible in the evening after a bright morning
Winter gale`s and frosts make us wonder about global warming
All to do with the Gulf Stream and El Nina forecasters explain
Who are all intent on never doing a "Michael Fish" again
High or low pressure reflected by the barometer on the wall
If the pressure is high it rises, if its low it will fall
Fir cones will close and smoke drift down if pressure is low
When pressure is high cones open and up the smoke will go
The colour of clouds whether white, black, light or dark grey
How high they are giving us an indication of weather on its way
Sometimes looking at the clouds will tell us all we need to know
If it will be wet or dry or if in winter it's likely to snow
Sometimes sunshine sometimes rain on the window pane
Wind direction easily checked with a look at the weather vane
Morning red sky shepherds warning, at night red sky shepherds delight
With our weather usually coming from the West this is invariably right
Now so many amateur weather watchers in this modern age
Eager to keep records with their own temperature or rain gauge.

A CUP OF TEA

The most refreshing beverage wherever you may be
Beyond a question of doubt is a cup of tea
This Earl Grey. Whoever he might be?
If he gives tea parties?   He has never invited me
So many varieties you can always try something new
The other day I had a cup of Typhoo
Oh! they say there is nothing like a cup of tea
Just ask those monkeys that advertised P G
There are some like Camomile
For genteel ladies whose little fingers stick out a mile
No matter where you might be
Nothing more pleasing than a cup of Tetley
When the weather is hot and you tend to perspire
The cure may well be a cup of Yorkshire
Or if you have just finished dining
Your choice may be a cup from Mr Twining
Or if it is a real thirst you are feeling
You may wish for a cup of Darjeeling
It is said you can beat a wife a carpet and a walnut tree
But the one thing you can`t beat, is a good cup of tea
Milk? First or last It is up to you
Added sugar, one lump or two
No matter what you are at or where you are
There is never anything better than a cup of char
So many varieties the number is untold
Doesn`t need to be hot can be drunk cold
Some of it is good with herbs and spiced
Said to be even better if it is iced
Sagan, Dailya, Assam, Masala or Moringa tea
White, Green and Black tea
Ginger, Lemon, Herbal or Peppermint tea
Whether it is from China, India or Malawi
There is nothing like a good cup of tea.

MERRY WIDOW

There was a merry widow from Diss
Virtuous, but thought susceptible to a kiss
On a rainy market day under her brolly
Gave shelter to a raunchy local character named Ollie
Their conduct exemplary nothing improper
Being aware of the presence of the local copper
She happily accepted the invitation for coffee
Conversation un-scrutinised carried on amiably
With many local topics to be debated
As still the rain had not abated
Ollie thinking the price of a cup was a fee
Took a chance and stroked the widows knee
She virtuous and good said "you are a disgrace"
The flat of her hand, slapped him across the face
In quick response Ollie dropped on his knee
Declaring honesty and propriety, forgiveness his plea
The widow replied it is for me, to choose what I like
Be sure it`s not you "so get on your bike".

WINDMILLS

Windmills, not long ago uncommon almost rare
But now there are windmills here there and everywhere
Both big and tall others short and small
Generating green energy for the benefit of us all
Long gone the original concept of grinding flour
The quest now is for electrical power
Funded by various conservation schemes grant aided
Seeing electricity supplies enhanced and upgraded
Whether tall commanding sentinels in white
Relentlessly turning creating energy day and night
Or less obtrusive supplying a more personal need
Within the grounds of the farms and houses they feed
Often augmenting solar panels on a south facing roof
Reducing living costs and enhancing property values, in truth
 For some a blot on the landscape obstructing the view
For others the use of technology, adopting what is new
Using only what nature provides alone
No reliance on any other fuel or products grown
Windmills the long the short or the tall
Harnessing nature for the benefit of us all.

ANSWER LIES

No matter how a farmer or gardener may toil
Be sure the answer lies in the soil
Experienced farmers and gardeners always know
Where on the farm or garden certain things will grow
On lighter sandy loams the rain will percolate away
Yet will be retained by soil sitting on clay
Trial and error teaching them what will suit
That for potatoes and cereals may not be best for fruit
Friends across the country with gardens different to mine
All due to variations in soil structure acidity and alkaline
While for most plants the preference is a sandy loam
There are others content with a clay subsoil for a home
Some plants prefer their roots are moist like the rose
Whilst others are less bothered about the garden hose
Chalky, stony and sandy ground that dries out quick
Without irrigation fails to grow plants strong and thick
The consistency of crockery clay or bricks for houses to be built
Far removed from the best crop growing Fenland silt
Sand and gravel for cementing and concreting houses and roads
Quarried and extracted from the earth in great lorry loads
All the foodstuffs we are all dependent upon for our health
Gold, diamonds and all minerals that are the basis of wealth
No matter what you do or have in life, how hard you toil
You can be pretty sure the answer lies in the soil.

DELUSIONS OF GRANDEUR

With delusions of grandeur now long gone
Content in a more humble moderate throng
No longer struggling forever with an if and a but
Now that my cloth is a less expensive cut
It was surely an accident of birth
Not born into an echelon to match my worth
Past friends now viewed from afar
As I ride in a humble modest priced car
No qualms that I am less of a snob
Now friends that speak, from a less cultured gob
Happy with big store or supermarket clothes
To hang with tailor made copies of Saville Rows
Blow Harrods, Claridges and the Ritz no excuse
Now Marks and Spark`s the Red Lion or Fox and Goose
Then on the railway first class across the land
Now on commuter trains squashed having to stand
Once Dom Perignon champagne and caviar
Scaled down to scampi and chips and Tesco cava
Oh! Those youthful expectations of Grandeur
Now a palate and expectations less selective and fewer
No more forever struggling to please
Now comfortable adjusting to new friends with ease
Intellectual pursuits followed understood or not
For the adoption of the role of educated bigot
No matter that parents were brought to their knees
By the cost of up-market private school fees
How much simpler life without a care
Without pretence and presentation of a superior air.

RIGHT TO ROAM

It is decreed the public have the right to roam
Fields of farmers and the aristocracy I treat as my own
Not for me any re-aligned path of the current day
If another is marked on an outdated ordnance survey
From the city or country no matter where
The whole countryside is my heritage to share
If I wish to wander over heath land and moor
Fields and pasture though knowledge of agriculture is poor
To view both ponds and a distant wood
Whether or not my understanding of nature is good
Less restriction is required not more
With complete freedom on both cliff top and seashore
To hang with restrictions that appear harsh
Let me go wherever, below seawall onto the marsh
Why should I not traverse beside the river or bog
And be denied seeing newts , toads or a frog
No matter whether planted with maize, barley or wheat
It should be my right to choose where I place my feet
Another of the things that increases my wrath
Is avoiding horse muck when I walk down a bridal path
No matter if I am a leisure walker exercising my dog
Or a professional rambler keeping a detailed log
But should anyone enter my garden, by the gate
Intruding on my privacy, I will chastise and get irate.

THE MISSUS AIN`T HERE

The missus she has gone and turned queer
They`ve got her in hospital, she ain`t here
Dunno what`s wrong with her, but she will be alright
Nurse reckons she`s strong willed and plenty of fight
The missus has gone and given us all a mighty scare
Never thought she would be the one for medical care
Always looked after every one, if they done what she said
Nobody should ever need a hospital bed
Don`t worry those doctors and nurses you can be sure
They will keep on working till they find a cure
They reckon they have got antibiotics and drugs
That can cure almost any disease or bugs
They keep giving her all sorts of medicine and pills
They reckon they`ve got stuff to cure everybody`s ills
When they give her stuff they watch and monitor
Take blood pressure and check temperature with a thermometer
They even use science fiction now in their detection
So they can cure any illness or rare infection
Nurses come from all over the world from foreign parts
But are full of caring kindness to the bottom of their hearts
I go to see her every day and sit at her bedside
Not too far to go only about half an hour`s ride
When she comes home won`t be able to do much, just rest
I will need to cook and clean and do my very best
Yes the missus she has gone and turned queer
They`ve taken her to hospital, she ain`t here.

CHANGE MY CAR?

Yes I know the clock`s been round and round
 Should I change or keep running it into the ground
I could be driving what people call an old banger
But were I to change I could be making a clanger
Like old man river it just keeps rolling along
And nothing much has ever gone wrong
With 175,000 miles or more
Can still do 100 mph with foot right on the floor.
Change to what? Something sporty, stylish and trendy
Comfort first or should it be Eco friendly
Now-a-days car`s rarely breakdown to be fair
But Lindsay say`s French and Italian ones often need more repair
Something sedate, conservative with modest insurance
Or more flamboyant displaying, still youthful exuberance
Hmmm, what a bonus a new guarantee
Years of motoring trouble free.
It used to be steering wheel, lights, brakes and a hooter
Now it`s all electronics governed by a computer
Rain sensor`s parking sensor`s direction finder`s and more
All sorts of new technology, I have never heard of before
Electric mirror`s and seats and innumerable security devices
Now unbelievably to be had at affordable prices
Everything monitored and data recorded
Secret`s revealed when the information is decoded
Nothing left to chance to create terror
Except the nut behind the wheel called," human error".
Some would say I have been left at the gate
If I didn`t have a personalised or recent plate
Would a new registration fill me with elation or would frustration mount
When, I viewed the difference in the bank account
While pride and prestige may be heightened
One thing is for sure finances will be tightened.

DAYS GONE BY

Fond memories of carefree youthful days
With time to indulge in fun, frolics and irascible ways
Involved in escapades it would have been best to ignore
The camaraderie of friends, some deserving more
Young Farmers organised, nothing left to chance
Then gathering again for a Friday night dance
With events and opinion`s influencing life`s course
Decisions made "thought right", no cause for remorse
A life of twists, turns, glory days, heartache and tears
Now more sedately drifting into twilight years
Feelings and friendship`s some growing cold
Others remembered warmly as we grow old
Yet the truth of true friendship never lies
Always there unspoken revealed in the eyes.

Written after meeting a friend again after over forty years

"KEEP TROSHIN"

To hang with the un-bounding energy and extra gears
That have diminished with the advancing years
Just keep rolling on at a more moderate pace
Don`t let passing years, make you feel you have lost the race
Keep focussed, you are as young as you feel
Don`t give up remember there is no alternative deal
Never be kidded it`s time for idleness and shirking
Ignore the passing years keep active and working.
There will be times when things get a bit tough
Have a break now and then, but keep doing your stuff
The chance of regaining youthfulness is a forlorn hope
But it is no excuse for thinking you can no longer cope
Keep walking, bending and working day after day
Till eventually aches and pains have their say
Hips and knee joints don`t matter a Jot
Skilled surgeons on the NHS can replace the lot
No need to be in a hurry to meet your maker
The wonderful people in NHS will fit a pacemaker.

WINE

Oh! what better way to revive memories of a past time
Than with the enjoyment of a bottle of wine
Some may say when wine is in, truth`s out
Other`s may find fantasy runs a riot
Passion that can be inspired and inflamed
Control of faculties lost, wine blamed
Fun and enjoyment entertainingly heightened
In some, tempers less easily constrained
Amorous encounters that were never vetted
That often when sober become regretted
Only if it was not for the enjoyable taste
There are those that would have remained chaste.
For most the accompaniment to the enjoyment of food
The relaxation from stress and tension is good
At parties as an aid in making people socialize
Providing tolerance of others they may well despise
Creating jovial humour and banter a party atmosphere
Open discussion, gossip and philosophies rarely sincere
To the connoisseur an extension of the food`s flavour
An excitement for the taste buds to savour
With a circular motion it is judged for smell
Sipped to linger on the tongue as the flavour`s dwell
A serious selection for the accompaniment of a dish
Whether it be Game, Fowl, Meat or Fish.

GOOD WINES AND GOOD WOMEN
All my life I have been told a good woman is like a good wine, A
statement I have accepted and never questioned until recently whilst
cooking, and idly reading the blurb on the back of a bottle where it
stated something about best when drunk and further down it also
said best kept horizontal.

[90]

INNER THOUGHTS

Hidden in a secret corner of the mind un-fussed
A lifetime in seclusion having never been discussed
Historic memories and poetic licence entwined
The fuel inspiring a creative ancient mind
Now other forces that have no explanation
Unseen for fifty years, still providing inspiration
No need to doubt it defies explanation is true
While it highlights something special about you
The passing of years, the fantasies of the mind
Always reflecting on what was happy and kind
Would an old man's heart beat a little faster?
Or fantasies of years past reveal a disaster?
Questions and answers searched for, but unfound
In a mind stable active and perfectly sound
Long lasting memories that are sweet and kind
Forever tucked away in a secret corner of the mind
But you may wonder what it says about me
Have no fears, I have always, and still live happily
Those happy memories and feelings I had then
Now revealed by my actions with the pen.

GERTRUDE

Oh! Why didn`t I fall in love with you when I should
If I had I know life would have been good
I wonder if in my youth my heart was cold
That it is only in later life my truth is told
It is honesty to let it be known
I should have harvested those seeds once sown
Oh! "Gertrude" if you only knew
How in later life I often thought of you
Some recognise the real love of their life without care
Others like me failed, how life is unfair
Now I am near the end of my road
Wondering if I should have listened to what I was told
 It is only now I speak with an authoritative voice
With regard to having made the right choice
Was I the victim of my own ego
Determined no one would tell me where to go
What could the effects have been on my life
If I had had the wisdom to choose you for a wife
Would it have presented other opportunities to choose
Or predicted circumstances that were sure to lose
In reality life has followed it`s destined course
Dictated by my own decisions so no need for remorse
Realising now is too little too late
Should I have been wiser at the starting gate
Sad it is only now I put this into rhyme
Should have been wider awake at the right time.

'Gertrude's name has been changed

WINTER

Winter starts with December, the month designated for celebrating
Deciduous trees and hedges bare, animals and insects hibernating
The time when winter sports and indoor pursuits make their mark
Denuded trees revealing the beauty of a landscape looking stark
Carol singing and bells ringing in the Christmas celebration
Even if only for one day peace and goodwill across the nation
Cards to and from friends and relations, it is right we remember
Earmarking the most important and sentimental month December
Christmas day indulgence of food and the consumption of ales
Before purse strings are loosened for some at Boxing day sales
Time when critical self-analysis and good intentions have their say
Lifestyle improvements and resolutions made on New Year`s day
Weather often likely to be cold, dull, dour and damp
Whatever you are doing in daylight hours you need a lamp
Washing hanging on the line for hours, it`s called wash day blues
Best put it on radiators or in the tumble drier if you choose
At times coat and gloves needed for a walk in the crisp winter air
Followed by the welcoming warmth of a fireside chair
The garden dormant giving us weeks of freedom from toil
Supplanted by the constant use of domestic heating oil
Grass not growing cattle now housed in their winter digs
On sandy land no such luck for free range outdoor pigs
Fear of frosty mornings and ice, drivers needing to take care
Maybe a need for winter clothing perhaps thermal underwear
County Councils with tonnes of salt for the frozen roads
All of little interest to hibernating frogs and toads
It may be Global warming and possibly I am tempting fate
To even mention that winters have been milder of late
Never a better time to fully appreciate a fireside glow
Than in those winters when it chooses to snow
Children enjoy the excitement of toboggans and sleighs

Less fun for wildlife with squirrels confined to their dray`s
The sight of snow covered hives has one wondering about bees
And creatures hibernating underground or in hollowed out trees
Time moves on towards February with increasing hours of daylight
Crocuses, snowdrops and daffodils emerging in the wake of the aconite.

MINCE PIES

It is all good cheer as December arrives
Fuelled by great expectations and Mince Pies
Oh! Yes it is the universal treat
The first symbol of Christmas we meet
There are recipes galore
All shielded in mythological folklore
Each unrecorded and prepared rule of the thumb
Handed down every generation to a daughter by her mum
If offered one, eat every crumb, not one to be wasted
The provider is convinced it`s the best ever tasted
You may have had some earlier, your stomach extended
But do not refuse, for your host will be offended.

CHRISTMAS FARE

A penny for your thoughts? Angel on High
Now that food waste fortnight is nigh
With supermarket trolleys   filled to the brim
Never mentioned in any carol or hymn
The delicatessen counter piled with goodies galore
From every conceivable exotic foreign shore
Luxury foods too innumerable to mention including nuts
Some with the propensity to upset your guts
A fruit bowl full, of Grapes, Oranges, Apples and Pears
Tins of Biscuits and Quality Street in the cupboard under the stairs
To hang with the midriff bulge
It's time to over indulge
In addition to turkey, Christmas pudding, Stilton and port
Oh! How Christmas gluttony is akin to a sport
Cold turkey, ham with pickled onions and chutney is fine
Accompanied by lettuce, tomato, cucumber and another glass or two
of wine
Christmas cake, chocolates and mince pies
Turkish Delight, Twiglets and other essential buys
Oh! A penny for your thoughts? Angel on high
Now that food waste fortnight is nigh
For a beneficiary, may I make the suggestion
The company that manufactures cures for indigestion.

YULETIDE

Once again we approach that time of year
When thoughts of friends and family put our mind into gear
No matter whether being remembered with a card or gift
We admit either giving or receiving gives our moral a lift
For some of us, past Christmases may be yearned
With purchases made more comfortably with what we earned
Youngster`s looking for I-pads, blackberry`s or a play station
Without regard for falls in living standards or inflation
But nothing matches the friendship, wellbeing and good will
Providing it fits comfortably within the funds for the bill
And that great mystery of the Christmas tale
A card from aunt who? From where? Courtesy of the Royal mail
Wishing us "Bon Voyage" and good cheer
We promise to visit, to keep our conscience clear
All part of Christmases, noetic power of correction
Designed to make us question our own wayward direction
For some culmination of time spent on extortion and profiteering
Yet granted acceptance with good will by us the God fearing
There are those for whom hectic party going is nigh
Others to extend a hand to those, the World has passed by.

MERRY CHRISTMAS - 2015

Again we welcome Christmas, in its glory
How we always enjoy this wonderful story
First related by some romantic stranger
About a couple whose first born was in a manger
An uncomplicated story, that is un-fussed
Leaving the whole world with hope and trust
At first heralded as a revelation
Now the subject of a massive celebration
Time for religion, friends and remembering
With feasting together in a family gathering
With our homes lit up with a festive glow
Appreciation of friends and neighbours, we show
In a world savagely divided and blighted
Christmas attempts to make us more united.

SANTA'S NIGHT

With the Christmas moon shining bright
Reindeer pulling the sleigh with all their might
Santa is looking anxious and forlorn
Toys to deliver, a page in his address book torn
A difficult job now more of a test
Every parcel to deliver before the chance of a rest
Spec-savers glasses for the labels he has to read
The sleigh fitted with Sat-nav to increase his speed
Ensuring he never makes a wrong turn
Enough hay to give the reindeer energy to burn
Round every corner, town street and farm track
The job to be done while the night`s still black
Whether Trump, EU or Brexit he doesn`t give a hoot
Too many chimneys, getting clogged with soot
At long last the sleigh is getting lighter
Dawn is breaking the sky getting brighter
Hours to Christmas Dinner, the reindeer their oats and hay
Then like other older folk, sleep the afternoon away.

CHRISTMASTIDE

December brings the wonder of Christmas lights
Providing joy and cheer to dark winter nights
A time for remembering with peaceful camaraderie
The combination of carol singing and joyous revelry
When thoughts of gluttony begin to glint in our eyes
Purchasing a tin of quality street and sampling mince pies
The time for sending cards and exchanging gifts
Sometimes healing and at others creating family rifts
Children filled with excitement playing with new toys
Often it's drink fuelled raucous adults making a noise
Mothers and fathers in kitchens undertaking a culinary feat
Cooking a Christmas dinner with all the trimmings for us all to eat
Turkey, sprouts, parsnips, roast potatoes eating more than we should
But still not content we top it off with trifle or Christmas pud
Festivities cast away on Boxing day other things dominating thoughts
Some bargain hunting at sales others a full programme of sports
Our sincere best wishes for a happy and prosperous New Year
Tempered by atrocities in other lands creating trepidation and fear.

BAH! HUMBUG

It`s that time of year
For false friendships and good cheer
Furniture moved. Not as it should be
Just so we can have a blinking Xmas tree
Hanging around all day till nearly five
Just waiting for the postman to arrive
Relations who annoy me to be endured
While the drink, I purchased gets poured
Carefully selected presents pushed aside
By family members I can`t abide
They are all here, to enjoy my binge
Some with table manners that make me cringe
Unruly teenagers who think I should be proud
To see them prancing about and playing music so loud
Who wants to pull cracker`s and wear, paper hats
And act like adolescent brats
Thank goodness it`s only once a year
The rest of the time, a quiet corner, and a good beer.

MISERY GUTS

On my misery guts list there are a few
Can you be sure one of them isn`t you
Have you ever refused to do
That crazy invitation extended to you
Are you stubborn and dig your heels in like a mule
Lest a family member or colleague thinks you a fool
Every person has their own story
Some complacent reflecting in their own glory
Living a life that is sedate and slow
Setting standards they will not fall below
Others defy their age not facing the truth
Trying to recapture the spirit of lost youth
Up for challenges, adventures and high jinks
Regardless of what staid friends or the World thinks
Do that or go there you should have done it years ago
Prophets of gloom tell you, you are too old and slow
A misery guts wife saying don`t eat or drink that
It could upset your stomach or make you fat
That`s the sound of many an autocratic wife
Who feels it her duty to ensure her husband`s life
At parties to recapture. with rock-n'-roll or a twist
Nobody wants to know, they reckon it`s youth missed
But worse the husband who won`t be bossed
Won`t go anywhere or buy anything because of the cost.

SPRING

Moving from Winter to Spring, nature's most exciting road
With shoots emerging and early colours beginning to explode
Cautiously, hesitatingly fearing Winter may have a last fling
Early flowers blossoming and birds starting to sing
Lengthening days onward towards the Spring Equinox
Promise of Summertime at March's end, we change the clocks
When the morning chorus is the most welcome of sounds
Overwintering migrants returning to their breeding grounds
Sometimes some discomfort with March winds or April showers
But knowing the reward will be a profusion of May flowers
So many Spring sights we welcome with thanks
None more than seeing primroses in roadside ditch banks
Trees and hedges having once again become green
Bluebells and hawthorn blossom an encouraging scene
The sight of Easter lambs is rated amongst the best
Along with birds flying backwards and forwards to a nest
If it's a sunny Easter it will fuel Summer dreams
At beauty spots if the van is present, queues for ice creams
The sight and sound from high in the trees of rooks and crows
Grass growing, cows happily returning to the meadows
 Fertilising and spraying crops for the harvest already planned
Cultivations for vegetables in fields and gardens across the land
With the heaviest winter coat no longer needing to be worn
Time to start thinking about when we will have to cut the lawn
At Aintree the Grand National the World leading steeplechase
And on the Thames the unique Cambridge and Oxford boat race
Bedding plants for garden or tubs planted fingers crossed
It's still not too late to be caught out with frost
From mid-April watching for the sight of swallows in the sky
On brighter days we may be lucky to see an early butterfly
Cricketers and other enthusiasts preparing for Summer sports

But best keep a pullover handy still too early for shorts
Spring ends with the merry, merry month of May
Not just one but two Monday`s designated as a Bank holiday.

SOPHIE
(Now Kieran`s Fiance')

Congratulations Sophie on becoming twenty one
Celebrations to include a night of revelry and fun
Never one to have been tucked under anyone`s wing
Now officially free to choose the song you sing
Not for you rushing about frivolously and madly
Always there to give help, when needed gladly
Life`s main highway stretch`s out as you stand on the verge
Unaware of what opportunities and fortune may emerge
But ahead lies life`s tortuous road mile after mile
Waiting for you to complete with glamour and style
A utopian life is one very few are lucky to find
To most the tedium of work, with an occasional lift of the blind
Sophie whatever goals and challenges you have to face
You are sure to accomplish them with dignity and grace.

HAPPY BIRTHDAY, KIERAN
(Much loved grandson)

Kieran now that you are twenty one
Manhood fully reached, life still just begun
As you preview the prospects for your life
Incurring the responsibilities of a partner or wife
While still possessing all the spirit of youth
Now judged accountable for decisions, that`s truth
Yes! While still young enough to enjoy a fling
No longer guarded under any parents wing.
Now not the young kid on the block
Moulding yourself to become as solid as a rock
Your youthful exuberance will now blend
Like a shepherd, the needs of others you will tend
Lessons learned in your formative years
Creating wariness heartache and tears
Building on those years just spent learning
The confidence and self-assurance you were yearning.
Look forward to a future that is clear and bright
Opportunities to be grabbed when they are in sight
All through life the wind of change will blow
Creating Changes no clairvoyant could ever know
As the old grow older and slacken their pace
You are there, climb the ladder and fill the place
Visions for the future historically unimpaired
 Make your opinions carefully, and tactfully aired.
I am maybe not one to stand out in a crowd
Yet Kieran you make me Justifiably proud
Kind, thoughtful considerate and sincere
Making it a pleasure to have you near
With many prizes out there to be won
Hopefully your life, will be a long and happy one.

AND SO TO SLEEP

On the go from the break of dawn
The evening punctuated by the ever stifling of a yawn
Now is the time for that sleep I yearn
But all I do is toss and turn
Oh! for some restful slumber.
Not counting sheep of an indefinite number
Re-living the past day`s events more and more
If I could sleep, I would not mind, if I was to snore
Even a sleep that is light and not all it seems
The ever active mind conjuring up obscure dreams
Until I am finally unwound
And blessed with an hour or two that is sound
Now awake there is a bright morning sky
Time to get up, when I could just lie and lie.

GOLDEN RAINBOW

That rainbow on the horizon, is there a pot of gold
Or a story best left untouched and untold
Were I to journey to the rainbow`s end, across that field
Would it be a pot of gold? Or disappointment revealed
Could that pot of gold supply freedom and wealth
Do I already have it, being blessed with good health
If there was to be gold at the rainbows end
Could it be richer than the company of a good friend
Would a pot of gold satisfying lust and greed
Better honest endeavour and friends meeting every need.

THE NAZE

As I sit looking out to sea with a steady gaze
From the cliff top at Walton-on-the Naze
Thinking of the Worlds ever changing scene
with thoughts of those who sail the ocean green
Remembering mysteries told of days gone by
Before there were aeroplanes to fly
Countries now a playground for the wealthy to seek fun
Lands blessed with sandy beaches and plenty of sun
Others more ugly and torn apart by fear
With continual wars causing deaths year after year
The mighty sea its approach`s to lands carefully sounded
Container ships carrying cargo`s without fear of being grounded
Bringing clothes and white goods from countries far away
Landed at Felixstowe or Harwich for distribution across the U K
Supplying us with goods undreamed of in centuries before
Others seeing the surface and seabed as an energy source to explore
The ebb and flow of the tide perpetual motion of the sea
Yet man unable to harness this greatest source of energy
How I wonder at the seas never ending power
As the tides come in or recede hour after hour
Sometimes idyllic at others a vicious taskmaster nobody would wish
Endangering those whose lives depend on the sea, catching fish
Great refrigerated trawlers fishing in a way others are unable to match
Not leaving traditional inshore men enough to catch
For some a coastal cruise visiting ports, nothing is finer
For others it is like being in a sardine tin on a cruise liner
Which-ever,   is it the way to beat off the blues?
Being imprisoned in a floating luxury hotel on a cruise?
Passenger ferries sailing back and forth with goods
Some with refrigerated containers with perishable foods
Massive oil tankers bringing in oil from countries afar

Enabling our transport system, our lives dependent on the car
Sailing boats, yachts, motor cruisers and various craft for pleasure
All providing recreation with memories to treasure
As they face the wind and currents with skilled navigation
As befits the tradition of our peoples seafaring nation
Sea birds wheeling and circling rarely stopping to rest
Searching for food sources that is their never ending quest
Some of my minds thoughts as I sit and Gaze
At the sea from the cliff top at Walton-on-the Naze.

OLD FOGEY LAND

How life growing up was once so grand
 In what to me is now, old "Fogey" land
Younger generations disinterested in OAP folklore
Ones like me "forty years removed" considered a bore
Time passes and the world moves on
Parents and places inspirational once, now altered or gone
Infra-structure changing with new hands at the helm
 Landscape altered, diseased trees oak, ash and Dutch elm
Farms changed, less livestock more fields without gates
Even where modern technology lies, nature still has its way
There is not a one whose hair has not turned grey
Some fortunate showing signs of wealth
Others more concerned with struggles for health
Hearing aids and eyes that cannot stand glare
Needing long handled shoe-horns and a rising chair
Restricted diets and a box of pills
Central heating turned up for fear of chills
Creaking joints full of aches and pain
Giving advance warning of forthcoming rain
Yet always the concept on which the World evolves
It is children and grand-children around which the World revolves
 New technology not understood, like the I-pod`s youngsters yearn
And other mysteries us old Fogey`s will never learn
They have it mastered as soon as it is in their grasp
Not long ago it was our minds, as sharp as a rasp
But how the comforts of old "fogey" land abound
With the memories of people and places that are found.

RETIREMENT

Now that my working days are done
Time to relax and have some fun
No rushing why there is no need
Time to sit still with a book to read
Enjoy the pleasure of life free from strife
Visit the supermarket, push the trolley for the wife
Places to visit, friends to go and see
Time to sit and laugh over a cup of tea
The gardens tidy not much to do
"Come on dear". We will go and wander round B&Q
Walking, swimming bowls and golf all take up time
In the summer trips to the coast are sublime
Stopping off at a pub or restaurant for a leisurely meal
Throughout the week, on a cheaper pensioner`s deal
No need to stop at home and hide
With a free bus pass, can travel far and wide
No matter what or where it might be
There is likely to be a cheaper rate for an OAP
But not everything is as it should be
Will have to pay for Sky to watch cricket on TV
Just have to keep on watching the news
Run the country? "Hadn`t realised I had such strong views
Write letters to newspaper editors, and join the queue
To become the nation`s number one "Victor Meldrew."

SIRENS

Awakened by emergency sirens wailing out
 Is it Police, Ambulance or Firemen answering a shout
The Police to a fracas a traffic accident or affray
They need to be there for order to be restored without delay
Or maybe an Ambulance racing out blaring it`s horn
Somebody seriously ill or a baby struggling to be born
Whatever it may be, clear a path get out of the way
The emergency service needs to be there without delay
Speed is the essence must not waste time
As the Police endeavour to combat all manner of crime
The fire brigade responding to whatever the emergency
A fire an accident, a horse in a ditch a cat up a tree
The ambulance with paramedic for treatment that is vital
As it speeds its way, lights flashing to the hospital
Alerting road users with their sirens and flashing light
On standby always ready any time day or night
Yes the emergency services for ever on call
 Often unappreciated, but always there for us all.

NO NEED GENERATION

(Those of us born in the pre and post war period have experienced
one of the most prosperous periods in history)
A population aged and secure without need
Retired living on pensions, some tantamount to greed
Some, final salary plus or better index linked
When negotiated no raised eyebrows, nobody blinked
Generations blessed by a goose that laid a golden egg
Yet in spite of good fortune still some beg
Successive governments laws passed for social welfare
Raising state pensions. Tax credits and free health care
Houses furnished, wardrobes full, expenses low
Biggest problem what to buy where to go
Enough for everyone to meet their need
Except for those suffering jealousy and greed
Now the generation, no longer working, not needed
Able to give volumes of advice, but rarely heeded
Any not cared for with problems are relatively few
As charities and social services struggle to give them their due.

PENSION POWER

Pension power is the number that are there to vote
Pension power that is the phrase politicians like to quote
Happy pensioners to be seen out shopping without fail
For all sorts of goodies paying cash on the nail
 With time for leisure and pleasure it`s just grand
The less fortunate ones, the community gives a hand
For many they say there is nothing finer
Than going cruising on an ocean liner
Others nurturing plants and watching them flower
Is creditably their passion and pension power
Past an age when miscreant activities will bring disgrace
Life moving sedately at a determined relaxed pace
The energy in a pension power battery is not so large
Worst of all is the time it takes to recharge.

BREXIT

A life of blessings that have been mixed
Something`s broken that still remain unfixed
Culmination of circumstances or an event
Sowing the seeds for unrest and discontent
Something thought of as an inspirational tonic
Now a different scenario and questionable, if economic
Creating needs to be more flexible and pliable
For continued existence to be viable
How easy to become a Luddite and resist change
Not recognising a future with an ever widening range
What`s gone is gone never to be seen again
But how did I vote Leave or Remain.

Uhm!   Things rarely as good as you hope, or as bad as you fear.

FOOD

All sorts of variations that may pass our lips
From Cordon bluer to Sausage egg and chips
Exclusive dishes exotically prepared leaving taste buds thrilled
In summertime informal barbecues with meat char grilled
Meals that can be meat and vegetables stir fried with rice
The flavours controlled by wine. Peppers, herbs and spice
Culinary achievements of both great chef's and wives
Utilizing all manner of garden produce including chives
Delicacies with aromas to stir the palette and presentation to fill the eye
Yet struggling against the smell of a sausage, bacon and egg breakfast fry
So many flavours that can be blended and marinated to be tasty
Before cooking and serving in a crusty pastry
A plethora of foods to be enjoyed displaying taste bud flair
Not to mention jam tarts, Eccles cakes or a chocolate éclair
But hard to beat our national dish of fish and chips
Universally a favourite on almost everybody's lips
Less popular to-day dishes based on bread and yeast
Now with flavours of China, India and all over the Far East
Beef, mutton, chicken or pork stewed as a casserole
Challenged by batter pudding and sausage, "toad in the hole"
Carrots, Mushrooms and onions adding flavour to a pie
Served with potatoes, beans, cabbage or broccoli
Lettuce, tomato, cucumber and a slice of ham
A cup of tea accompanied by bread and butter with jam
TV chefs showing how deliciously extravagant it can be
While others display simple recipes, sugar or salt free
Yet above the rest the meal which satisfies the most
Is unquestionably our traditional Sunday roast.

THE DISS HAGGIS

With whiskery ginger hair and solidly built
Enquiring eyes of a highlander wearing a kilt
A Scottish highland gillie traditionally dressed
To recapture escaped Haggis his unstated quest
Unbelievably the escaped Haggis so far south
Recently spotted near to the, Diss Mere`s mouth
The Haggis with movement, surprisingly fleet
Were quickly at the other end of Mere Street
The gillie`s search for the chieftains of the pudding race!
Now mingling with the throng on the market place
The gillie`s undoubted canny stalking skill
Soon cut off any escape up Pump Hill
Having spied and enlisted a Norfolk country lass
Dispatched her to frustrate any attempt at St Nicholas
The Saracens Head chef, with culinary expertise
Stood in Mount Street waiting his opportunity to seize
Folks on foot to Chapel Street and cars turning left
Any escape route there looked bereft
 Church and churchyard the fear of ghosts far reached
With memories of what "Robert Burns" once preached
Spotting the only open door at that end of town
The Haggis rushed in, and there stood Butcher Browne.

(Browne`s sell haggis sent down from Scotland)

NORFOLK

With its vista`s of expansive landscapes to fill the eye
And many varied churches reaching into the sky
From Kings Lynn to Gt Yarmouth the land is good
Well farmed supplying the nation with food
Equally the fertile soil from Cromer down to Diss
All easy working, productive ,a farmers bliss
Downham Market the edge of the Fens, land as good as you get
To Hunstanton and Burnham Market, the domain of the Chelsea set
Historic houses, Blickling, Holkam and Houghton,
rewards of those most loyal
Now overshadowed by Sandringham,
the symbol of everything Royal.
The county among the most renowned for retirement and leisure
The Broads and Coastal resorts where thousands come for pleasure
From Wroxham to Potter Heigham and the rivers Bure and Yare
Along the coast where-ever you look tourist attractions are there
In the south west the land of the Brecks, is Thetford Forest
Much undisturbed, a haven for wildlife, nature at its best
For over wintering and migrating birds you needn`t think twice
The North Norfolk coastal marshes a bird watchers paradise
Graced by Norwich a fine city, where technology is among the best
Only bettered by Cambridge just a little to the west
As a shopping centre Norwich regarded amongst the elite
But I am no judge, shopping an area where I drag my rural feet.

NOSEY PARKERS

Nosey Parkers, not just neighbours of all shapes and sizes
Government and community officials, using surveys as their disguises
It used to be just a curtain twitcher next door
Now government's big brother, monitoring your lifestyle and more
Not content with knowing how many people live in your house
They want to know if the woman you were talking to, is your spouse
Dear sir important to take time to complete our survey
Then all your personal details will have come our way
How can we tell if it's a government or local spy
When every department thinks it has a right to pry
National insurance, tax, passport and medical records they hold
On confidential secure data bases, not to be revealed we are told
You may think you live a hermit like existence on your own
But on data bases galore you are there and known
With CCTV in streets, shops and all public places
And sophisticated technology to recognise the faces
There is little or nothing the beggars don't know
With satellites in the sky to check what crops farmers grow
Oh! Please just complete our survey, we won't tell
Our aim is to target you with goods we have to sell
Can I ask did you borrow, you may have a PPI claim
Lining our own pockets, that's the name of the game
Telephone forever ringing with voices supposed to be banned
About prizes won or bank problems, so you can be scammed.

A PHEASANT'S LIFE

Not for me, a nest by a hedge sheltered with thorn
Never had a mum, in an incubator I was born
Brought up warm and dry with water and rearing crumbs
Even if not brothers or sisters, lots of chums
As I grew older I was left to acclimatise
Then separated into smaller hutches and pens on size
Never had to scrap or hide in the hedge out of danger
Just waited to be fed by the head ranger
Always watched so we could not crowd or smother
Monitored to be sure we were not pecking one another
As time went on we grew and grew
Then split into smaller groups two by two
A life stress free I never had a growing pain
Always a nice shed for shelter should it rain
Even without freedom I did not have a care
Growing up in a pen with plenty of fresh air
Until getting my Colours, size and weight
Given freedom having to survive in the wild, my fate
Oh how! I relished the freedom to roam
In my wild and natural home
Never before experiencing predators having to be wary
life now more unpredictable and scary
Survival of the fittest no longer a sheltered community
A creature of the wild responsible for my own immunity
Learning that staying in woods and fields was safer by far
If I ventured on to roads, could get hit by a car
Till hounded by beaters with sticks, and flying off in surprise
Only to be shot at by some "rotter" wishing me as his prize.

SATURDAY MORNING SHOPPERS

Canny Saturday morning shoppers with an eye for value
I welcome the chance to pass the time of day with you
As we search the aisles for bargains galore
Supposedly on shelves from top to bottom across the store
With popular products placed at eye level height
Not a guarantee that it is the price, that's right
How I wonder do we waste pounds (£) by the score
Are the best values either on the top shelf or the floor
Buy one get one free, not what we need
Unless we have additional mouths to feed
All that attractive packaging , to catch the eye
Tempting but the decision is, do we want to buy
Fruit and veg selected after a lot of thought
A week later little eaten, been better not bought
How gullible are we to physiological trickery
Led by smell, buying unwanted bread at the bakery
No matter how complicated our culinary expertise
All equally provided for, as is bread and cheese
For meat and dairy no need to think twice
Thought needed for oriental dishes cooked with rice
Rarely giving any thought for a ready meal
Yet always being sure not to run out of breakfast cereal
Realisation that whatever we put in the trolley
At the cash tills we end up spending lolly
Be comforted as we push our trolley to the door
That the prices are fair, with a card for match and more.

OUR JEAN

On Saturday mornings she is likely to be there
Her weekly shopping being done with consideration and care
From section to section she steadily goes
After a cautious start with lettuce and tomatoes
Carefully on selecting a variety of fruit and veg
With a shrewd eye for quality and a lifetime's knowledge
Sometimes meeting someone she knows and passing the time
Into the next aisle and maybe a bottle or carton of wine
To biscuits, crisps, chocolates and sweets
Like all grannies she keeps a score of treats
With her lightness of foot and complexion so fair
Shopping on with deliberation, confidence and care
The bakery, sugar, tea, coffee and breakfast cereal
All sorts of other ingredients to make or compliment a meal
Sometimes something a bit fancy at others more plain
Depending on whether she is having guests to entertain
Chicken, beef. pork, dairy products whatever she needs to buy
All under the close scrutiny of her all seeing eye
With frozen foods and cleaning materials the trolley has it's fill
Time to look for the shortest queue to pay at the till
Now fully stocked with a week's supply
It is time to say till next week, Mr Morrison Good Bye.

COURTNEY

Courtney a bonnie lass so blithe and fair
Ambition uncomplicated with an unpretentious air
Enjoying your youth with freedom and passion
Interests covering friendships, culture and fashion
School and college both met face to face
Easing past both with style and grace
Life`s focus may be diverse, but parents remain a priority
Even though it`s a situation of divided loyalty
Learning early how not to be at cross swords
Now prepared with the eloquence of chosen words
A desire for a life on a sound foundation built
Free of restriction, recrimination or guilt
A future firm and stable if not necessarily grand
But free from the fluctuation of shifting sand
With journalistic skills and freedom of the press
You are on the road to making life a success
Story`s and history recorded by the power of the pen
Of events that have happened both now and then
The opportunity and expectations the World can offer you
Chance to enjoy the kaleidoscope of its panoramic view
Ambition with the realisation there is a World to travel
With journalistic qualifications a future will unravel
Thoughts that are generated in an ever roving mind
Sometimes pure fiction at others a benefit for mankind
Not for you dalliances with any unworthy suitor
Preferring to seek a virtuous and more artistic future
Born with determination and ambition of goals to achieve
Confident of picking the right steps as through life you weave
With fond memories of your formative years
Always Joyous yet sometimes disrupted by tears
Learning that life is ruled by conditions you must abide

I have been on the sidelines watching you adjust with pride
No matter how life evolves as time goes by
I will be a grandfather with an understanding eye.

AFTER SUPPER

Culinary achievement's enjoyed with flavour and hope
Tempered by a digestive system that struggles to cope
A palate that for years faced challenges undaunted
Forever reminding of limitations not to be flaunted
The passing years determining our fate
It is only plain dull foods that should be ate
Those that are adventurous and never learn a lesson
Are advised not to complain if they suffer indigestion.

(Written after a very good Haggis party)

SUFFOLK

The county famed for Newmarket, centre of the horse racing sport
And Felixstowe, the home of the country`s largest container port
Largely a farming county with sugar beet, potatoes, cereals and rape
A musical culture of the highest order with the concert hall at Snape
A coastline that extends a warm welcome to those seeking pleasure
With historic finds at Dallinghoo, Hoxne and Sutton Hoo of treasure
History of Cardinal Wolsey, St Edmund and flint knapping at Grimes caves
Not to mention erosion of the coast, and Dunwich the town under the waves
Suffolk sheep the great wool trade and the churches they chose to build
Lavenham for centuries the centre and home of the wool making guild
To the South there is Constable country where Suffolk and Essex meet
And Long Melford credited with England`s longest village street
In the North the Waveney valley with unheralded scenic beauty and charm
Rising in a sanctuary for wildlife epitomising its tranquillity and calm
Picturesque villages with ancient houses wood framed and roofs thatched
Areas of World War two airfields from where bombers were dispatched
Still RAF Lakenheath, where the USA air force has a base with air power
Hopefully enough to keep the peace and make most nations cower
A county once known for Ransomes Sims and Jeffries threshing machines
Now its Framlingham`s Ed Sheeran, the "pop idol" of girls in their teens
Bury St Edmunds with its cathedral the county`s second largest town
Historically important when Edmund, king of the Angles had his crown
The Elveden memorial for those A11 travellers a most welcome sight
Remembering those locally dying in wars, fighting with all their might
Ipswich the county town and the point where all the main roads meet
A12 London South and North to Lowestoft once of the great herring fleet
As well as Minsmere Heath where the BBC film Spring Watch for TV
Which is practically next door to the nuclear power station Sizewell B
Retirement towns of Southwold, Aldeburgh and Felixstowe by the coast
The Orwell bridge serving two highways A12 and A14 its proud boast
A14 Felixstowe to Midlands and A140 to Norwich through agricultural land

Varying quality some heavy, some loamy some not much more than sand
Ipswich the centre where administration and commerce are at its heart
Whilst recognising the contributions of Constable and Gainsborough to art
Gone the days of Ramsey and Robson and the highest realms of sport
Now sailing on the Orwell or Deben or perhaps golf a more likely thought.

WHY

A World so varied in culture and belief
Almost as diverse as its geographic relief
Each with a religion depicting a tribal inheritance
With Gods representing many a differing stance
The countries of our birth many untold
 Will represent the religious views we hold
Each in essence presenting a moral code
For those wherever to travel life`s road
Sadly though it is not uncommon news
A struggle for power over different religious views
If true that Gods power rules our heart
Why are some in the World intent on us pulling apart.

ACLE STRAIGHT

Efforts to improve the Acle straight are to no avail.
Until relocation of the Little Whirlpool Ramshorn snail.
Be patient road improvers there is no hurry.
Apart from the Acle Straight it is only found in Surrey.
 If more Human life`s are lost it is a poor old do.
Important the Little Whirlpool Ramshorns are not too few.
No doubt in our existence, it has a part to play.
Please ecologists tell me in which way.

EDP 22nd October 2016:
Acle Straight to be delayed for four years because of snails.

HARRY`S WIFE

Harry Horringer from Hartest
Never one to be regarded as the smartest
Like his father rat catching was his trade
His wife probably Suffolk`s ugliest maid
With squint eyes a twisted mouth and a button nose
Always dressed in cheap ill-fitting clothes
Knock kneed and pigeon toed
Hadn`t a clue of any fashionable mode
An only child Molly Melford was her mother
Well seen, why she hadn`t risked another
ump and round shouldered with a twisted bust Amazing she even
inspired Harry`s lust
Yet only fair the whole truth be told
When it came to kindness, she had a heart of gold.

DEVELOPMENT

Memories of years gone by long since erased
Of grass fields where cows and sheep once grazed
Country cottages where families of ten or twelve once grew
Now rarely occupied by more than one or two
Fields that grew barley, oats, turnips and wheat
Now covered with houses, buildings and concrete
Council planners with the unenviable task
Of making recommendations on the applications folks ask
Housing shortage? The very words urban sprawl
Suggest there should be more than enough houses for all
Surprising how much of our green and pleasant land
Has permissions undeveloped on designated building land
The challenge of getting applications approved and granted
In the areas where it is most needed and wanted
Decisions and recommendations for approval often a close call
With many differing opinions, impossible to please all
Often it seems luddites and historians need little excuse
To oppose any ideas and applications for change of use
A lot of the planners work hardly worth a mention
Consisting of no more than a home improvement or extension
Out of town office blocks and industrial estates
Likely subjects for long and protracted
New roads and realignment with improved safety planned
Needing compulsory purchase and acquisition of land
Wild life conservationists and environmental groups
Studies on insects and mammals make planners jump through hoops
Authorities aware of community recreational needs for good measure
Providing golf courses and other facilities for residents leisure
The public always checking to see what applications are on the card
Not really worried, unless it happens to be in their back yard.

SUPERMARKETS

Supermarkets filled with folks for evermore
No matter where you look across the shop floor
For their shopping, some ladies dress up to the nines
Before parading up and down the lines
Sometimes a gent, in a suit overdressed for the part
Looking as though he has never let off a fart
Perhaps their morale is boosted by sartorial elegance
Only matched by the colour of the flowers and plants
They may be en-route to another function that beckons
And have just popped in for a few seconds
For most though it`s ordinary every day clothes
As they fill their trolley with Veg, cornflakes and loaves
Mothers with young children doing their weekly chore
With rampant children collecting things across the store
Just like Santa`s little "Elves", they soon empty the shelves
Whilst others considering ourselves more urbane
Select goods cautiously from whichever lane
Examining every turnip, parsnip or stick of celery
To ensure it`s free of any natural blemish there may be
Is our nutrition based on dieticians of the Jamie Oliver creed
Or more on our basic palate and sometimes greed
Goods in our trolley selected with discrimination and stealth
Influenced by those pundits promoting longevity and health
Newspapers in the trolley can tell a tale
Traditional conservatives, it may be the Mail
Those more interested in sport, sex and fun
Line their trolley with a copy of the Sun
Those with the Times and Telegraph
May give you a polite smile but rarely laugh
All across the shop floor it`s folks free of vices
Only focussed on which are the best prices
No matter whether a bearded Wally or dressed to kill
All get treated equally when they reach the till.

NORFOLK HILLS

If I am ever to see those Norfolk Hills
I will need to take stronger and stronger pills
The sign said Saham Hills, so I tried
Then looking at the map, How Hill I spied
Such a name touched a few chords
Investigation revealed a house by the Broad`s
The Broad`s of course are more like a lake
And the whole darned place as flat as a pancake
Grapes Hill now that`s in the city
Just houses and traffic what a pity
Ashill sounds as though it should be seen
But turns out to be as level as a bowling green
But all is not lost, do not give up hope
There is a few places if it snows, to toboggan down a slope
Wondered at the thought when I heard of Castle Rising
But it is only a few feet above sea level, not surprising
Names Like Alby Hill, Gold Hill and Frog Hill appealed
When visited as flat as the arable acres around Westfield
It Will need more potent and stronger pills
If I am ever going to see Norfolk Hills.

CHARTWELL

The passing of time and the coming of age
Heralding the pensioners making a pilgrimage
Many with memories and stories to tell
What better place for a visit than Chartwell
Many with anecdotes of times gone by
Of sirens and warplanes filling the sky
Now the intent of those raider's from far afield
Lost in the serenity of the views across the weald
Some with walking sticks and arthritis to the fore
Recalling earlier events of those years of war
Gratefully expressing appreciation, so well deserved
For the years when the nation was so well served
Pre-war politics that had caused attitudes to harden
Resulting in the overwhelming glory of the garden
The perseverance that the nation should not fall
Commemorated in the building of that garden wall
The challenge of fighting to defeat Hitler's power
Paling into in- significance to the beauty of flower
The determination that inspired the nations will
That is how we remember Winston Spencer Churchill.

A FARMING LAD (1937-20??)

A farming lad born and bred
Life spent working to ensure the nation was fed
Always eager to be playing a part
First job's still with a horse and cart
The Ministry of Agriculture encouraging production evermore
With tractors, sprayers and chemicals the yields did soar
Woods and hedges scrubbed, fields made bigger
Increased production and efficiency the trigger
Year after year was a record breaker
With more wheat, barley and sugar beet per acre
No matter what it was you planted in a field
It was paramount to choose a variety to increase yield
Year in year out prices remained stable
Subsidies ensuring cheap food on the nation's table
Whether arable or livestock, production advanced
Enabling profitability to be maintained if not enhanced
Livestock enterprises and breeding just the same
Faster genetic progress always the name of the game
Bigger machines and efficiency always on the increase
Feeding evermore people in offices, some becoming obese
Introduction of European dictatorship to stem the tide
With payment for unfarmed land to be in Set Aside
systemic and organic methods with added virtues implied
Alongside modern technology of genetically modified
Now bedevilled by lower returns and ever increasing inflation
Farmers opening farm shops and other forms of diversification
Land values increasing at a rate second to none
With never an indication of the strife that was to come
Today with fields full of solar panels galore
Worldwide integration, politics and prices on the floor
For generations housing and land values have been the reward

Providing collateral on which new developments are anchored
Some grasping and developing what they think will be obtainable
With many older heads shaking, and questioning if its sustainable.

SUMMER

Even if not the hottest it heralds the years longest day
Months when the country`s sun worshippers get their say
Far removed from Winter`s darkest days of gloom
Of all the months it`s June that sees Britain in full bloom
Salads and other garden produce providing us with energy
The cold of Winter with cetral heating now a distant memory
Wherever you look, county shows to village fetes are planned
Open gardens for charities and family barbecues across the land
Some days hot and humid when we would welcome a breeze
As one potters or just sits in the garden in shorts and shirt sleeves
Or perhaps family memories with sunshine again come to the fore
With time spent relaxing with a picnic on a beach at the seashore
The chance to fulfil Winter`s dream of lounging in a deck chair
Best to remember sun cream however if your complexion is fair
In horse racing both Royal Ascot and Epsom derby day
The time when weather has to be right to make the best hay
Garden centres supplying plants and materials a demand hard to meet
For colourful hanging baskets adorning town homes and the village st
reet
For some Wimbledon fortnight complete with strawberries and cream
Others a week`s sailing at Cowes regatta fulfilling their dream
Garden`s at their most beautiful as they promised when in bud
With music festival goers hoping for a Glastonbury free of mud
Flower beds needing weeding, lawns to be cut and edged
Garden hedges trimmed now any newly hatched birds have fledged
School holidays, increased numbers travelling to foreign lands
Air fares and hotel room prices elevated to their highest bands
The local tourist industry over years has been nurtured and built
Accommodation of all types by the sea, or broads cruisers full to the
hilt
Pick your own fruits with those country fresh flavours to savour

For immediate consumption, freezing or jam making with your own labour
Corn and rape seed crops bred for earlier harvesting and increased yield
Combine harvesters now with over forty foot swathes soon clearing a field
With day`s now getting shorter and outdoor maintenance jobs well in hand
Holiday makers are retuning mostly looking healthy and well tanned.

TREES OUR HERITAGE

What in the summer would be a cooling breeze
Now a cold blast blowing through winter's trees
That great Oak looking forward to centuries more
Having withstood the ravages of the centuries before
Alongside where once stood mighty Elm trees
Before they were blighted and lost to that Dutch disease
Never seen an artist's landscape not enhanced over time
Among those often chosen, Ash, Birch, Cedar or Lime
Trees have customised town streets including Park Lane
Whether it be with Birch, Poplar, Sycamore or Plane
In the country another farm name we often see
Is the one which records the presence of a Walnut tree
In the summertime what better place to watch a river flow
Than from under the hanging branches of a weeping Willow
Wooded hills and valleys making an endearing view
Often churchyards providing a home for the poisonous Yew
Another favourite without any if, or a but
The dominance of the magnificent Horse chestnut
Not forgetting fruit trees in orchards tended with care
Providing us with varieties of cherries, plums, apples and pear
Life embellished by our traditional trees mostly all deciduous
Now complimented with many ornamental some coniferous.

WALKING

Roadways, footpaths and tracks
All well-trodden by keep fit anoraks
By rivers, across fields mile after mile
Lanes and bridleways sometimes going over a stile
Pressure is on to keep fit with a regular ramble
Even down a muddy path overgrown by bramble
Day in day out across the heath
Delaying the day our name is on a wreath
Following scenic routes on quiet roads and byway`s
Away from the hub hub of the main highways
Through wooded glades and parkland
On little used routes that centuries have spanned
Many with a long forgotten purpose
Leading from hamlet to workplace or church
Believing walking and exercise makes us "healthier" by far.
Didn`t people die younger, before the age of the motor car?

UNSPOKEN WORDS

(Some thoughts on an early girlfriend, happily married, who I have met again after over 40 years)

Things that were to be
Or not to be
The truth sometimes hidden or lied
Or cast away by a rushing tide
All that glittered not gold
Leaving worth wile values cold
Could and should
If not for a head of wood
Eyes don`t tell lies
Alternatives determined by fate
Realisation coming too late
Of all the minds in the land
One I would wish to understand
Now nothing to alter the tone
Left are only memories alone
To ascertain no one else will ever find
Hidden in a darkened corner of the mind.

MY MORNING CHORUS

It is worthy of the wait all night long
To hear the sound of the early morning bird song
My blackbird is usually first of all
Waking everybody with his strident early morning call
Setting a standard to follow that is a must
With others soon singing their lungs fit to bust
I toss and turn, my first partially stifled yawn
Lost to the bird song welcoming the new morn
Along with the pigeons cooing and the pheasants cackle
Heralding the day we have all yet to tackle
The robin the thrush, finches and tits all join the natter
Each convinced they have a voice that should matter
The birds in the morning chorus are a mixed blend
Staking claims to territory that is theirs to defend
Or for some it is the desire to search for a mate
Time for them to relinquish their bachelor state
Knowing it`s another day they are being put to the test
For a search for food is their never ending quest.

POETIC LICENCE

Poetic licence a powerful fuel to remember
It can fan a flame from any smouldering ember
Recalling the exuberance of youthful days
A lifetime of differing interests changing our ways
Lifestyle interests and values adjusted by circumstances
Far removed from that envisaged in an early romance
Governed by efforts deployed to create wealth
Yet always overruled by the need to ensure health
In a world where we are not all the equal of others
Although it is preached we treat them as brothers
Life is adjusting to an ever changing game
Leaving behind luddites who wish to stay the same
Accepting technological advances and the utilisation of time
Replacing tasks that were laborious and covered by grime
Long gone the chance of change and correction
A lifetime remembered with fondness and affection
Regardless of any changes that may be immense
All easily disregarded with poetic licence.

SOCIETY DEMANDS

Blood sweat and tears
For goodness knows how many years
With every effort to honour promises made
Benefitting the family and ensuring taxes are paid
Through hard times when vision seems blurred
On meeting the commitments that have been incurred
Family or business decisions taken on lightly
Requiring additional work efforts almost nightly
A lifetime that demands a constant work ethic
Year in year out, sometimes becoming hectic
Never any suggestion you should be acclaimed
Aware society demands social levels are maintained
Keeping head down taking care not to fall below
Standards determined to be the neighbourhood status quo
That the local community has established a moral code
That you are beholding to maintain and never erode
You learnt the rules and how to conform
Taking care to never to go beyond the norm
But not till the family is fledged and grown
Are you able to harvest the seeds you have sown
Gradually it becomes clear that everything is not ongoing
With nature telling you that you are slowing
Now worn on the wrist a copper band
For the sake of arthritis in the knee or hand
Looming ahead retirement and your only need
Dead heading roses and searching flower beds for a weed.

VOYAGE OF LIFE

The intrigue of that ship or person that passed, as if in the night
Positively steered? Or drifting? Oblivious but now out of sight
I wonder of their survival and fortune in life`s tortuous course
In whatever way nature may have administered it`s force
Some battered and bullied, lashed by life`s tide
Others well preserved and cared for sailing on with pride
For there is never any guarantee that all will be well
As we struggle to cope with life`s ever changing   swell
A lifetime for some as if in the doldrums and becalmed
Others lashed by a storm force, lucky if unharmed
Some reaching twilight enjoying life as if in a tranquil bay
Others challenged by illness and diseases wanting their way
Oh! That ship or person that passed, as if in the night
We are unlikely to know of their fortune or plight.

ME

Am I what I am
 Or am I what I have become
Am I what I should have been
Am I what I could have been
Am I an addition on the scene
Am I best to remain unseen?

Written for a friend after his wife died

A FRIEND

When God saw you tired and ready to go
He reached out and touched your pillow
Wrapping his arms around you
He whispered come unto me.
Much as we relished your friendship and charm
We respect God-given peace and freedom from harm
Whilst a loss the family will mourn
Now into Gods kingdom you are truly born
Those fortunate to be within your mixed blend
Were privileged to regard you, as a friend
Eternal life on earth was never to be
Yet you will live forever in our memory.

TOO EARLY

(Another who died young)

We have been dealt a hefty blow
You were far too young to go
You a flower that was still much in bloom
Have been picked far too soon
May be only the good die young
If we believe the song that is sung
It was a shock and surprise to us all
Learning that you had received your call
Although now into Gods kingdom you are truly born
Leaving a tragedy for the family to mourn
The Lord chose to reach for your hand
But you had much to give before joining his band
Lord you may seem to have a rare find
To those left your taking is cruel and unkind
Forgive us Lord for all these tears
We will have the absence for many years
If those taken early are truly blessed
Why are those left so severely stressed
It may be said that is what was meant to be
But you will live forever in our memory.

THE HEALTH LOTTERY

It is not in our power to choose
Who amongst us will win or lose
Some have an active immune system that comes into play
In others undesirable genes dominate the DNA
You can be assured that the passing of the years
Will see friends and neighbours suffering, bringing forth tears
With little imagination of what is contained in our DNA
We have no idea what pain and suffering may be on its way
Health and lifestyle gurus give us boxes to fill with ticks
In their attempts to work out how to reduce the risks
Across the World, hospitals are amongst the busiest scenes
As they struggle to combat our unsavoury genes
Public and charity donations fuel research and development
To aid advanced technology for new treatment
Media pundits are intent to criticize imperfections in the NHS
Which is to be commended as a victim of its own success
Pharmaceutical giants manufacture masses of pills
To control and stabilise so many differing ills
Doctors and nurses working longer hours at their station
Are truly the lifeblood of the nation
For most lifestyle and health are not theirs to choose
Some with tobacco, drugs and alcohol light their own fuse
And increasingly gluttony is playing its part
Especially with conditions associated with cancer and the heart
It is right those in good health appreciate it every single day
As we witness those where disease and disability is having its way
No matter whether lifestyle makes you a saint or sinner
If you have good health as you age, you are a health lottery winner.

OUR GREAT GAME

Those who can kick balls and run like hounds
Can get salaries way beyond normal bounds
Managers and players arrive and depart in a never ending flow
Almost totally dependent on the way results go
From around the World of every race colour or creed
Players striving to satisfy the games unquestionable greed
Locally whether a Norfolk yellow or a Suffolk blue
Your allegiance to one or other is likely to be true
Delia Smith cooks with consistent results
Even if on Saturday her team reveal a few faults
Whilst Marcus appears to be an owner without a care
For the most part nobody knows if he is ever there
Over the years the teams have had legends galore
Either as resolute defenders or forwards able to score
Both clubs with memories that will forever last
Of great achievements and personalities of years past
It appears that it is results more than style or fashion
That inspires the supporter's commitment and passion
Each week the emotions of the fans in the stands
Sometimes elated and cheering at others with heads in their hands
Let us not forget the school playground where it all begun
And in those minor leagues people playing just for fun
Yes years ago in schools and on streets the seeds were sown
And every team with talent that was home grown
Fortunate are those to have reached great heights
And feature in Match of the Day on Saturday nights.

BYWAYS

Main routes and highways best ignored
With many lanes and by roads to be explored
Down a country lane from a town usually just a short hop
Where a converted barn or cowshed is now a farm shop
By farm houses and country cottages signs Horses go slow
Probably or like the ones I lost money on years ago
Another sign often a subject of the Sunday motorist`s quest
Free range eggs, after all they are supposed to be the best
A wandering country by-way not sure where it goes
Doesn`t matter much if at the farm shop you got potatoes
Continually slowing down for walkers some with dogs
Passing other houses selling either kindling or logs
In various fields the chance for you to compare
Crops of wheat, barley, sugar beet or maize growing there
By-ways offer a varied scenic route
Plenty of pheasants and game if there is an organised shoot
Sometimes the glimpse of a flight of ducks from country ponds
Always a rewarding sight for those with rural bonds
Sparse population and woodland providing wildlife cover to hide
The few houses there, looked after with considerable pride
Clearly it is gardening or at least so it seems
That is an integral part of every ones rural dreams
Away from the highway, by-ways have an infinite charm
Only if tractor comes the other way is there cause for alarm.

DAIRY EXODUS

Off to the West, Norfolk's dairy cows do go
All because the price for milk is too low
Changes in our countryside, as the herds are lost
As farmers struggle to produce milk at an economic cost
Throughout the country the picture is much the same
With Milk buyer's and supermarket's the ones to blame
Bigger herds and investment in efficiency in efforts to keep pace
Only resulting in returns on capital that are a disgrace.
Better genetics and management continually increasing milk flow
Cited by consumer groups and milk buyers for profits being low
The quest for higher productivity a never ending race
Year in year out only to find yourself in the same place
The commitment of dairy farmer's is hard to believe
Missing the animals and interest is what they will grieve
Working Bank holiday's and Sunday's never a chore
They would willingly keep doing it if paid a bit more
Sale catalogues state sold to change in farming policy
Easily interpreted as meaning lack of profitability.
 Supermarket's say their profits are not what they used to be
At one time a four pint bottle was one pound fifty three (£)
The current price has now been trimmed
Now for a pound you can buy four pints of semi skimmed
With little done to promote milk with beneficial recipes
Regardless of Dairy Co and their imposed levies
Now more farmers are converting to arable
With milk production no longer viable
There is no doubt Norfolk agriculture is not what it used to be
With departing cows leaving Norfolk air almost methane free.

*(My figures reveal 235 farms producing milk in Norfolk in 1995 now
about 30)*

GRACES

For the last few years I have been doing graces for the local
Holstein and Jersey cattle club dinners. Here are four I quite like.

Grace

You are welcomed here tonight
To celebrate the black and white
Cows forever bred to increase yields
As they graze sun kissed meadows and fields
The champion of all dairy breeds
Providing dairy products the nation needs
A blessing for those with culinary expertise
Whether it be milk, butter, yogurt or cheese
 It is our privilege in giving thanks for this feed
 To honour and celebrate the Holstein breed.
Amen

Grace

We are gathered to honour the island breed
The Jersey cow that satisfies our every need
From her beginning on an island so small
She has spread across the World conquering all
Full-filling every culinary experts dream
Producing milk, butter, yogurt and cream
Of all the cattle breeds she is the one most able
To supply the luxury required at the top table
In giving thanks tonight for this feed
We honour and celebrate the Jersey breed.
Amen

Grace

Some are enthused by the tractor and the plough
Others driven by the love of the dairy cow
We are gathered here all of the same ilk
Our common interest the production of milk
Our numbers are forever getting fewer
If only we had prices more stable and secure
But no matter Trump, Brexit or EU
The Holstein cow will see us through
Tonight our troubles forgotten as we enjoy this feed
We are here to celebrate the Holstein breed.
Amen

Grace

If you require the dairy cow to meet every need
You have no further to look than the Jersey breed
There is a long list of traits in which it will excel
Economy of production milk quality and conformation as well
Not only does she produce the milk with the richest flavour
She has the looks and charm that even royalty savour
There is not one to match the famous island breed
When it comes to cows of whatever race colour or creed
Yes tonight we honour and celebrate the Jersey breed.
Amen

AGED AND UNWANTED

The aged and unwanted, in this modern technological age
The ability to retain the necessary knowledge difficult to gauge
As the fast moving digital world reveals its realistic truth
Adjusting and adapting to change is much easier for youth
Delegated to the next generation the challenge of modernistic skills
Older folks often sticking to traditional methods and a "box of pills"
Less reliance on experience or the written words of any bard
Knowledge on a computer, heralding the changing of the guard
Gone the days when digital technology resembled a victory sign
Now it can control cookers, heating and other appliances on line
With internet banking by phone, and bank closures planned
Bad news for those relying on cheque books and cash in hand
Outdoors in the sky surveillance being carried out by drones
In factories workers replaced by robots working like clones
Smart phones, tablets, touch screens giving business a new dimension
Hold complexities and fears of being scammed by some on a pension
Some grand parents have embraced the digital revolution
With families and grand-children in faraway places, Skype is the
solution
Tele-communications keep developing at such a fantastic pace
Little doubt to some of the aged it is a new and unwanted face.

COMPUTERS

When it comes to computer`s I am not very bright
It`s off to One Two One, Mary soon puts me right
Attentive she listens and identifies my needs
Sells me the right gadget complete with connecting leads
My study a mass of plugs and wires, that`s the truth
Designed only to be understood by a youth
Connect printer instructions followed to the letter, "Won`t work"
Ring Mary patience exemplary, never say`s "Done it wrong you jerk"
Advice given, left click here double right click there
Darned thing starts to go, "the Woman`s" an angel I swear
On her advice everything done at first hand
Got myself signed up and connected to Broadband
Always impressed work done, be backed on a disk
If computer crashes would be lost, don`t take the risk
Needs explained, with confidence she says this is the very thing
Come out of the shop with something looking like a key ring
Plug it into USB apparently it is called a memory stick
Have to call Kieran to get it to work, "I am still too thick"
The computer a necessity, informative and fun
But what a nightmare without Mary at One Two One.

FIFTY ODD YEARS AGO

When life went with a swing
We had the Beatles and Stones songs to sing
When arthritis hadn't been invented
And the digestive system was contented
Fifty odd years ago
There were things to do, not to be missed
On Saturday nights we danced the twist
Out of the house all alone
No computer or mobile phone
Fifty odd years ago
 With Peter Cook and Dudley Moore, Monty Python
And That Was The Week That Was, they were on
Concorde had just taken to the air
And what about the Profumo affair
 The Great Train Robber's they had a go
Fifty odd years ago
Opportunities to make a fortune scorned
But yet never mourned
Decisions and actions that seemed right at the time
Although some turned out less than sublime
Fifty odd years ago
 Now that attitudes and ways are set
There is nothing to regret
 But the truth has to be told
Now that I am to ruddy old
Of opportunities missed
Ladies who should have been kissed
Fifty odd years ago.

TIBBENHAM TREACLE MINES

In years gone by the County's punishment for crimes
 Could have been days working in Tibbenham treacle mines
When prisoners from the surrounding jails
Were marched to the mines carrying their pails
Mines now extinct were situated on the parish's Northern edge
Where the village topography turned to scrub and sedge
Yes it was this part of the parish then most hated
That the treacle digging industry was located
With the prisoners forced to work long hours
 Whether it was cold with rain or even snow showers
Extraction which always proved difficult and tricky
The consistency of the treacle when it surfaced sticky
Making the winter collections always more viable
The treacle being less runny and more pliable
The harvesting which was done in open cast mines
Was always located using garden forks with four tine's
Before being carefully scooped up and put in the pail
Ready to be refined put into jars and sold retail.

POET

I am a no good poet
And I know it
It only has to be a reflection of the times
And it is likely to get a mention in my rhymes
There can only be one thing worse
To be not even considered for a verse
Anything thought to be controversial news
Is likely to attract my diverse abstract views
No matter whether national or local
If passions are stirred reactions may be vocal
Yes no doubt if it draws my attention
I will be moved to give it thought and a mention
Subjects on which many would not give a curse
My twisted mind may well come up with a verse
There are those of you who will jump up and shout
 Poor devil should have something better to think about
Disoriented thoughts more in common with a goat
Than one writing verse in the manner of a poet.

AUGUST

August the month of my birth
When harvests reveal the year's true worth
With apples, pears, plums and cherries
Not to mention a plethora of other various berries
Usually blessed with warm sunny days
Yet nights sometimes reminding us of autumnal ways
Farmers are only intent on getting their harvest in hand
Other's only objective, to get sun kissed bodies tanned
While farmer's may be thinking wheat, barley and oats
Some have thoughts of hiking, swimming and sailing boats
Yes with school holidays it is time too for leisure
With outings and trips designed to give pleasure
At week-ends holiday routes clogged with traffic queues
The evening air often carrying wafting smells of barbecues
Seaside amusements and fairgrounds continually manned
As beaches get evermore footprints on their sand
With more and more flying to exotic destinations by air
To air conditioned hotels full to capacity when they get there
Now cricket is no longer just an afternoon in the park
With coloured balls and floodlights it can be played after dark
Yes now even after your head has hit the pillow
You may hear the sound of a ball being struck by willow
A month when both farmer's and sportsmen exercise their right
To make use of every daylight hour and even into the night
And it's here again seemingly without any reason
All too soon the start of the new football season
For those whose passion is sport with a gun
August the twelfth is the day grouse shooting is begun
t is also the month designated for parliamentary recess
Allowing politicians to absent themselves from duties regardless
As the month ends, the heady days of summer are receding

We become aware of the autumnal changes that are impeding
Witnessing swallows and other birds preparing for continental flights
And indoors we find an ever increasing need for lights.

WIND OF CHANGE

The wind of change does continually blow
Leading to a future we will surely never know
Each year the months and seasons once again
Sometimes warmer sometimes colder or more rain
Our lives more unregulated and less climatic
Yet more uncertain and sometimes dramatic
Times of opportunities providing reason for hope
At others difficulties have us wondering if we can cope
Many fortunate to find a golden way on life`s path
While others bear the brunt of ill health and life`s wrath
Some driven by the ever increasing demand for wealth
Others happily blessed with contentment and good health.
In science and technology advances almost by the hour
Aimed at improving health, wealth and power
Almost from birth in children`s minds seeds are being sown
To increase and expand the knowledge that is known
Research and development moving at an ever increasing pace
To benefit both health and prosperity for the human race
The winds of change that have blown evermore
Creating a driving force for mankind to continually explore
In industry and travel winds of change continually blow
Many rural bus services amongst things that no longer go
With solar panels and evermore wind farms mainly at sea
Now being utilized and exploited to provide electricity
In tomorrow`s world whatever will the changes be
As the wind of change in youngster`s minds run free.

LONER

A loner with a day spent in contentment alone
Un-encumbered in the company enjoyed most, their own
Unhindered with no one other than one`s self to please
Time unimportant able to adjust with ease
No need to fit, into a family's busy schedule
A life controlled by one`s individual module
Although there are other`s held dearly in the heart
Retaining the freedom to choose when they play apart
There may be neighbours either side of the garden fence
But there is no way it compromises independence
Not indifferent to the community and it`s welfare
Happy to choose how much one wishes to share
Not selfish will always willingly go to help others
Usually first to pick up the phone to sisters or brothers
Happier following one`s own preoccupations and dreams
Rather than constant involvement in organised teams
Life smooth running controlled and self-regulated
Interruptions and adjustments for others sometimes hated
Time spent in unbroken thought entirely on one`s own
Much valued, that mind and body have freedom to roam
A loner joining in whenever they choose is never alone
But the company enjoyed most is their own.

TRAINS

A sight in the far distance from my kitchen window
Trains on the London to Norwich line whichever way they go
A regular service throughout the day one about every hour
All running smoothly using overhead electrical power
Nine carriages in the middle and an engine at either end
Was only one, when coal was shovelled and a fire to tend
Commuters often unhappy complaining or so it would seem
Thank goodness they no longer have the nostalgic days of steam
Train operators and staff continually bickering it would seem
One wonders if it harks back to unrest in different times
When Beeching wielded his axe closing many uneconomic lines
With a number of different operating concessions across the land
At busy times still not enough seats, and people having to stand
Depending on where you are trains of differing colours will be seen
Operators choosing liveries whether it be red, white, blue or green
From city to city across the country in a near straight line
With embankments and cuttings built to minimise any incline
Bridges and arches over roads and highways, tunnels through hills
With speed and movement now controlled by electronic signals
Where road and rail meet there are level crossings on flat land
Flashing lights with barriers and gates, very few still manned
Across rural landscapes where there is deemed a social need
Trains will call at smaller stations never reaching any great speed
Junctions where routes converge and passengers may have to change
All a part of the nation's great railway network range
From ports and docks to depots across the country goods we all need
Goods trains a great length of containers that powerful engines haul
Sidings where at busy times freight trains will have to wait
Passenger trains with schedules to keep, best they are not late.

(The following are just a few of my large collection of absurdities)

UNUSUAL LAWS

United Kingdom
It is an offence to fall off the top of Blackpool Tower under any circumstances.

A lady cannot eat chocolates on a public conveyance.

A bed may not be hung out of the window.

It is illegal to die in the Houses of Parliament.

Germany
It is against the law to mention the year 1966 in any football ground.

It is illegal to allow your car to run out of fuel on the autobahn.

Switzerland
You may not wash your car on Sunday.

It is illegal to flush the toilet after 10PM.

France
It is illegal to kiss on the railways.

It is illegal to call a pig Napoleon.

Australia
In Victoria it is an offence not to get a qualified electrician to change a light bulb.

USA
Alabama: It is against the law to place an elephant in an electric oven. The use of motor boats on the city streets is forbidden.

And in Lee county selling peanuts after sundown on Wednesdays is illegal

Alaska: it illegal for donkeys to sleep in bath tubs

Oregon: It is illegal for a dead person to serve on a Jury

Maryland: You may not keep chickens in your hotel bedroom

QUIPS AND QUOTES

We sometimes get the information. But refuse to get the message.
You have gift share it, you have smile wear it.
Positive attitudes and negative thoughts have one thing in common: both are habits.
The gates of happiness swing on hinges of gratitude and generosity.
Learning to skate is like having a joint bank account it`s hard to keep your balance.
The greatest pleasure in life is doing what people say you can`t do.
Happiness is not a treasure we discover along the way. It`s an attitude we practice day by day.
Money still speaks louder than words, whether you make it the old fashioned way or inherit it.
You must make yourself happy, just like you make yourself anything else.
The only time a man admits his driving could be better is when he is talking about golf.
A pedestrian is somebody who thought there was a gallon left in the tank when the gauge said empty.
Ten minutes of good luck makes you forget all the bad luck you ever had.
You spend 18 months getting children to stand up and talk, and 18 years trying to get them to sit down and listen.
Why do people with a cough go to the theatre instead of the doctor.
Accept good advice gracefully, as long as it doesn`t interfere with what you intended to do in the first place.
Never itch for anything, you aren`t willing to scratch for.
When preparing to travel, lay out your clothes and money, take half the clothes and twice the money.
In a butcher`s shop a woman asked for a pound of sausages. They are kilos now said the butcher. 'Alright; said the woman, 'give me a pound of kilos'.

Ever noticed that food with half the calories, costs twice as much.

An intellectual is a person who uses more words than he needs, to say more than he knows.

It is hard to say when one generation ends and another begins, but it is somewhere around 9 or 10 clock at night.

No situation is so bad that losing your temper won`t make it worse.